LIFE
REPURPOSED

Destiny Image Books by Thom Gardner

*Growing Up Into Christ: A Study
in Integrated Spiritual Formation*

*Healing the Wounded Heart: Removing
Obstacles to Intimacy with God*

*The Healing Journey: An Interactive
Guide to Spiritual Wholeness*

*Living the God-Breathed Life:
An Invitation to Rest at the Table*

Relentless Love: Unfolding God's Passion, Presence, and Glory

LIFE
REPURPOSED

BRINGING GLORIOUS TREASURE OUT OF THE
WOUNDS, HURTS, & PAIN OF THE PAST

DR. THOMAS GARDNER

DESTINY IMAGE® PUBLISHERS, INC.

P.O. Box 310, Shippensburg, PA 17257-0310

"Publishing cutting-edge prophetic resources to supernaturally empower the body of Christ"

This book and all other Destiny Image and Destiny Image Fiction books are available at Christian bookstores and distributors worldwide.

For more information on foreign distributors, call 717-532-3040.

Reach us on the Internet: www.destinyimage.com.

ISBN 13 TP: 978-0-7684-5227-3
ISBN 13 eBook: 978-0-7684-5228-0
ISBN 13 HC: 978-0-7684-5230-3
ISBN 13 LP: 978-0-7684-5229-7

For Worldwide Distribution, Printed in the U.S.A.

1 2 3 4 5 6 7 8 / 27 26 25 24 23

Freight: _____

By: _____

Invoice Value	Weight	Total Units Ordered	Total Units This Shipment
235.83	18.80 lbs.	30	30

DEDICATION

We dedicate this book to our children,

our girls,

who have demonstrated

the repurposing grace of God

in our lives.

We love you,

always.

CONTENTS

INTRODUCTION

It was February 17, 2020. I had not been feeling well for several months and had traveled from specialist to specialist to diagnose what was going on in my physical body. On that Sunday afternoon, Carol insisted on taking me in to the hospital—against my will. Two hours after we got there, I stopped breathing. I was suspended between life and after life for seven days. It was discovered through the great care of skilled physicians that I had suffered encephalopathy or infection of the brain. After I came out of the coma, I was incapacitated and semi-conscious for a few more weeks. The next thing I knew, I had lost a month. When I came to full consciousness, I was shocked to discover it was closer to Easter. Due to my illness, I could no longer walk, stand, or even sit up in the bed. My right side was completely numb and my hands compromised. In total, I was in the hospital or rehab for two and a half months. Now almost two years later, I have regained some abilities with much left to do.

We might ask, what's the point of this story? Simply this: God has a purpose even for this. Since my illness, I've had to be transported most of the time in a wheel chair. I notice now when places say they are handicap accessible, they really aren't handicap accessible. I see the world through different eyes now. My own illness has given me increased compassion and awareness of others who are challenged. Every day now is a true gift of grace, the repurposing grace of God.

One of the frequent questions that arise out of various kinds of traumas and challenges or loss is, "Why?" Here's the problem. When we ask, "Why, God?" we exit the realm of the spirit and enter the realm of the mind. We discard the reality that God may have a purpose for whatever our circumstance or challenge is. Notice that I did not say that God caused this challenge. That would be heretical. But He will repurpose it if we are open and present to Him. Maybe we've lost a loved one or are presented with a difficult diagnosis. Perhaps we've lost a job or a marriage. The shards of our circumstances lie around us like pieces of broken pottery. We ask, "Why?" or "Why me?" We cry out, "God, where are You? Where did You go?" We may believe that God has abandoned us or that we've somehow moved beyond reach of His tender love and care. "Why, God?" We may question our identity and security in the love of God

Beloved, God has not moved. He has not changed His mind about us. Our identity as His beloved has not changed. A loving embrace awaits us in the healing arms of Jesus to resolve the lies ingested because of trauma and challenges. But there is more—much more. God *repurposes* our flops, failures, and wounds to bring further healing to us and to establish His presence in and through us. The apostle Paul wrote, "*I am of the opinion that there is no comparison between the pain of this present time and the glory which we will see in the future*" (Romans 8:18 BBE).

It is my prayer that the following chapters may be a map or a compass in the wilderness to help us find unexpected gold from our past trauma or present grief—to find a new vision and hope for the present and future. We will ask a few questions along the way:

- What does it mean to repurpose our lives?
- How do we learn to see with a new vision?

In this writing, we will define and explore the repurposing of our lives. As we present our broken pieces to the feet of the Great Repurposer, they will be transformed and infused with new purpose and power to bring release from captivity, passage through seemingly insurmountable obstacles, refreshing in the wilderness, and victory over spiritual enemies. More than anything else, our repurposed life will become evidence of God's amazing and *repurposing grace.*

The following chapters will reveal the repurposing grace of God in the lives of ordinary and imperfect people just like us. There will be a few stories from real people along the road of their journey who found the hidden treasure even in the wilderness. We will take inventory of our own lives and see foundations for hope filled with new possibilities as we find our *Life Repurposed.* Each chapter will include an opportunity to reflect on your own life in order to find the hidden treasure waiting to be repurposed in the hand of God. God is the Great Repurposer—the Craftsman of creation itself. Listen as He says to you, *"Behold, I am making all things new"* (Revelation 21:5).

It is suggested that the reader include the repurposing format used in this book as a normal spiritual practice. This is part of taking thoughts captive to the obedience of Christ. You will be encouraged to "Turn Aside" at the end of every chapter. You will find a pattern that instructs us to See, Turn, Open, and Present ourselves to the purpose of God.

Prayer of invitation:

Heavenly Father, I ask You for the grace to see, to turn aside, to open my heart, to present myself and my circumstances to Your presence and truth. And I yield myself to You now, in the strong name of Jesus.

Part I

Beyond the Wilderness

Graves into Gardens[1]

You turn mourning to dancing
You give beauty for ashes
You turn shame into glory
You're the only one who can
You turn mourning to dancing
You give beauty for ashes
You turn shame into glory
You're the only one who can
You turn graves into garden
You turn bones into armies
You turn seas into highways
You're the only one who can
You're the only one who can[2]

---

1 "Graves Into Gardens," lyrics © Be Essential Songs, Bethel Music
   Publishing, Maverick City Publishing Worldwide, Brandon Lake Music.
2 Author's note: It is suggested you listen to this song before reading
   the next chapters You Tube Link:

7

CHAPTER ONE

HIDDEN TREASURE UNDER OUR FEET

I will give you the treasures of darkness and hidden wealth of secret places, that you may know that it is I, the Lord, the God of Israel, who calls you by your name (Isaiah 45:3).

You and I are surrounded by hidden treasures. Such unmined treasures may lie around us like so much junk littering the landscape to be stepped over or ignored because we don't see their value and potential. These treasures hold power for healing and comfort, not only for us but for others around us if we could only learn to recognize them. You are likely standing amidst these great resources as you read these words. They are in plain sight around you even now. The treasures I'm speaking of are the brokenness, disappointments, even failures we've experienced in our times of personal wilderness past and present that may be invested with new purpose and value.

When we experience challenges, we may feel isolated and alone, even anxious. We may feel frozen and maybe a little trapped. We are experiencing the fog of war with an unseen enemy, and there is no certain time when this fog will lift. We cannot see what is in front of us.

DRIVING THROUGH THE FOG

Because I learned to drive in the flatlands of Illinois, I was not used to driving through the rolling hills and valleys of Pennsylvania where we now live. I learned that at certain times of the year, fog tends to settle between the many hills especially at night. It can be so thick that driving becomes an exercise in patience. Our hands grip the steering wheel more tightly and we strain our necks forward into the fog and peer into the translucence.

I remember Dad's words: "Thom, when you drive in the fog at night, you will be tempted to put on your high beam lights, but that will actually cause the fog to be worse because it reflects back to you. So when it's foggy, turn on your low-beams and slow down." This may not have been a verbatim of the lesson, but you get the idea. I recalled that lesson many times then and since. When I drive through the fog, Dad's word is still with me.

Dad's driving in the fog lesson is clear to me today in this foggy time. It still applies. I will speak for myself. When I'm in a fog of whatever type, I'm tempted to want to turn on my high beams and figure out what's around the next bend in the road. I'm human; it's what we all do. We are an impatient species. When there is a fog, I need to put on my low beams—that is, I need to pay attention to what is right in front of me and slow down.

So how might we all switch on our low beams and pay attention to what is in front of us? How might we slow down a bit? First, we can pay attention to the people with us and learn to be a little more present to each other. We can listen to one another, really listen. We can call someone else who has experienced difficulty. Turning on our low beams may be paying attention to who or what is in front of us—not getting too far ahead of ourselves and trying to strategize the next move. Who is in front of us? We can include our relationship with God. What is God doing right in front of us? Who might He lead us to connect or reconnect with?

When we are in such a fog, we may ask ourselves, how can we get out of this arid and untenable reality? In our wandering, we may feel fear or confusion, hopelessness. We may feel alone and overwhelmed when none of our familiar formulas for life seem to work. *It feels like wilderness—darkness.* How could anything good come from this? Yet there is hidden or unmined treasure beneath our feet at this moment.

In 2010, thirty-three miners were trapped 2,300 feet below ground in a mine cave-in. To the outside world there seemed very little hope of good to come from this tragedy. Yet God was doing something amazing as the entire world was fixed on this disaster for many days. In the midst of this crisis hidden in utter darkness, the light of Christ was shining from one humble common follower of Jesus Christ, José Henriquez. He wrote of the experience:

> As I took hold of what I had learned and began to talk to my companions about the Lord, God began to work in them and gave them an opportunity to know him and communicate with him. Some of them were immediately brought out of darkness, and with great joy I saw how the Lord was transforming their lives.[1]

There could have been no more precious treasure mined from the darkness than the light of Christ and transformed lives. The world was watching to see if or how these men might come out of the 70-day ordeal. The rescue from this particular wilderness got the attention of a fascinated world and hidden treasure came out the darkness. Regardless of the nature of our wilderness, God is ready to repurpose it and *bring treasure out of the darkness.*

TURNING ASIDE

Are there thoughts or memories of past challenges or preoccupations with present circumstances that rise to the surface from time to time like a beach ball in a swimming pool? Do you push them down under the water only to have them pop up again? Perhaps you've underestimated them. Take a few minutes and reflect on these buoyant thoughts and experiences. You may want to note a few of them on the lines that follow here or in your journal.

NOTE

1. José Henriquez, *Miracle in the Mine: One Man's Story of Strength and Survival in the Chilean Mines* (Grand Rapids, MI: Zondervan, 2011), 67-68.

CHAPTER TWO

LIFE REPURPOSED

That men may know from the rising to the setting of the sun that there is no one besides Me. I am the Lord, and there is no other, the One forming light and creating darkness, causing well-being and creating calamity; I am the Lord who does all these (Isaiah 45:6-7).

Many years ago when I was in college as a music education major, I took classes at two different campuses: Saint Vincent College in Latrobe and Seton Hill College in Greensburg, Pennsylvania. I commuted between campuses driving along a back country road along green rolling hills with a house here and a farm there along the way. I threw my trumpet case and books in the back seat of my white Karmann Ghia convertible and breathed in the fresh air with the top down (weather permitting, of course). The drive and scenery provided a little decompression and refreshment between classes and rehearsals.

On one of those days, I observed a spot along the route where someone had begun to pile up what looked like junk—a piece of lumber here, a window there, maybe a door or other odd building materials lying about. As months rolled by, I would occasionally see a middle-aged man dressed in an unexceptional way, steadily pushing a construction wheelbarrow filled with more junk up the hill or perhaps cleaning the mortar off old bricks or just organizing his heaps of what appeared to be junk.

He was assembling older, used building materials from who knows where—a demolished house or office building perhaps. There were windows and doors and pieces of metal, wood framing lumber. I'm sure he had to buy some new things, but basically he gathered building materials that apparently people didn't see as having much value or potential. The materials piled up over some time to become quite a collection. I recall feeling a little resentful of this man and his ad hoc junkyard. It was a real eyesore along an otherwise green and peaceful road. This irreverent treatment of the landscape lasted for many months, maybe a year.

I can't recall the total amount of time that elapsed, but what seemed like a random junkyard began to take on definite shape and purpose. One of those days on my drive, to my great surprise, a foundation for a small house emerged from the ground. As I watched over some time, recycled bricks became walls. Discarded doors and windows were refinished and installed to fit perfectly into what emerged from the heap to become a place to live!

That house still stands these many years later. The builder took what seemed to be a useless heap of cast-off debris and *repurposed* it to become a habitation. This anonymous man's house of repurposed materials could be a metaphor for life as well. The house is still there with a new owner. His repurposed house lives on.

WHAT IS REPURPOSING?

It has become popular to *repurpose* items ranging from old furniture to picture frames to farm tools and any number of other items. I once had dinner in a restaurant in Erie, Pennsylvania where the entrepreneur repurposed an old railroad passenger car to become the dining room. There have been entire TV programs devoted to refurbishing and decorating homes with repurposed pieces.

We live close to Pennsylvania Dutch country where it is not unusual to see somebody repurpose an old plow or some farm implement to become the centerpiece of their landscape surrounded by flowers and new life. Some visionary builders may use repurposed or reclaimed lumber from a dilapidated barn to build new furniture or decorate an accent wall of a new home. Not only are these repurposed pieces environmentally responsible, but they also bring character and depth to their new environment. My wife and I have a few repurposed pieces in our home.

To be repurposed is to see obsolete or unused items with a new vision and to infuse them with new life and adapt them to a new purpose. To repurpose disregarded resources requires imagination and artistry to see them with potential beyond the way they may have originally been conceived.

My wife, Carol, is a drama and English teacher. One of the productions she organized was of *The Lion, the Witch, and the Wardrobe* by C.S. Lewis. In her dramatic productions, Carol demonstrated the ability to see potential in items that others may not always see. In the production of the C.S. Lewis classic, Carol needed a large crown to adorn the head of the White Witch, but couldn't find one that fit this important character in the play. Then, while walking through a particular retail shop, she saw a wire wastebasket with the approximate dimension of the crown she envisioned on the brow of this sinister character. The bottom was removed and the rim lined and the whole piece was painted white. Where others saw a wastebasket, Carol saw a perfect crown.

My dad was another person who was a good *repurposer*. He had a great passion to adapt and repurpose old furniture or disregarded mechanical parts in his workshop. For instance, Dad repurposed baby food jars to hold an assortment of nuts and bolts and other bits of hardware and mounted them on wooden disks suspended from the ceiling on a spindle. Once, an electric motor from a discarded appliance was fixed to a flexible cable to become a sanding wheel. In all of the cases above, supposed obsolete artifacts were enlisted to new vision, purpose, and value-adding depth and beauty to those who repurposed them.

GOD THE CREATOR AND RE-CREATOR

The following verses describe God's self-disclosed repertoire of repurposing craftsmanship.

> *That men may know from the rising to the setting of the sun that there is no one besides Me. I am the Lord, and there is no other, the One forming light and creating darkness, causing well-being and creating calamity; I am the Lord who does all these* (Isaiah 45:6-7).

The keywords and images here are *forming* and *creating*. Both words describe something fashioned in the hand of the Craftsman of creation. Forming refers to something reshaped from existing material, while creating implies the bringing forth of something out of nothing. God does both. God forms and reshapes even the darkness to His purpose.

When we look at the context of the Scripture from Isaiah 45, it is clear that Isaiah was talking about a pagan king, Cyrus, who would not be born for many years after Isaiah's prophetic word. Cyrus would be repurposed to return the people of God to the ruined city of Jerusalem.

> *Thus says Cyrus king of Persia, "The Lord, the God of heaven, has given me all the kingdoms of the earth and He has appointed me to build Him a house in Jerusalem, which is in Judah. Whoever there is among you of all His people, may his God be with him! Let him go up to Jerusalem which*

is in Judah and rebuild the house of the Lord, the
God of Israel; He is the God who is in Jerusalem"
(Ezra 1:2-3).

The Lord, the God of Heaven, called this conquering king to transform a heap into a habitation for God and His people. Truly there is no God besides the Lord. God's creativity and re-creativity are boundless. It is who God is. His heart and creative nature are seen through every means we can imagine, even what looks to us like devastation.

A few years ago, Carol and I were in a forested area at the foothills of the Blue Mountains in New South Wales, Australia. There had been a terrible forest fire that had been reported in the media even as far away as the United States. We had visited the region many times and were interested to see the results of that destructive blaze. A friend knowledgeable in the things of nature drove us into the burned forest to observe the devastating result of the fire.

We were astonished to see what I thought was a species of tree. The forest was filled with trees that had blackened bark but were also surrounded by fresh, green life. I inquired, "What kind of tree is this with black bark and such green leaves?" My friend then unveiled the grand refreshing and repurposing work of God through nature, even fire. There were seeds pods on the bark of the trees that were broken open by the fire, spewing out seeds for new growth. The result was an amazing and surreal contrast of the black bark from the devastation of fire against the delicate green of fresh life. Because God can repurpose a fire to bring new life out of devastation, what else might we place at His feet?

God repurposes all the good, the bad, and the ugly as we release our lives into His hands in Christ. The apostle Paul, himself a repurposed persecutor of the church, wrote, *"Now we look inside, and what we see is that anyone united with the Messiah gets a fresh start, is created new. The old life is gone; a new life emerges!"* (2 Corinthians 5:17 MSG). In Christ we aren't just getting a new paint job—not a mere cosmetic makeover. In God's re-creative hand we are converted into something brand new—new nature, new identity, a new purpose.

It is important to know that as our past challenges or present circumstances are repurposed, we are not talking about renovation or remodeling. Something new is coming forth in the hand of God. Everyone who belongs to Christ—who has put their lives, with all of the challenges or griefs or failures, at His disposal—is becoming brand new.

GOD SEES POTENTIAL WE DON'T SEE

God, the Artist and Craftsman of creation and re-creation, often rummages through the broken and disregarded pieces of our lives to repurpose them into something that will bring Him glory. He sees something in our wanderings that we may not see. We have all faced, or may be facing now, various kinds of challenges along life's road. We may see them as I saw what appeared to be a heap of junk along my drive those years ago. We may have written them off as an interruption to spoil the scenery of our journey. But these repurposed pieces teach us. They soften us. They speak to us and through us of God's repurposing grace.

In our ministry, we have often used pieces of a Japanese art form called *kintsugi* to illustrate the value of repurposing. Hundreds of years ago a powerful Japanese emperor entrusted a precious broken vessel to a craftsman for repair. He chose a unique adhesive to reconstruct the vessel. The broken shards were put together with gold. Now, what began as a piece of pottery became a far more precious work of art. So the Craftsman of Heaven often puts our broken pieces together with the gold of His repurposing grace, making us new creations in Christ.

As we journey with God, we need to think about our challenges differently. Might God have a purpose beyond healing? Can we place cancer or some other serious illness at His disposal? Can a traumatic event become an open doorway to redirect our lives? We must move beyond an explanation of suffering in which we ask "Why?" and into asking, "What's next?" The shift happens as we find the heart and presence of God rather than what He might do for us. It is a shift toward maturity.

When we first come to Christ, we are interested in what God might do for us. But as we mature in that relationship, we become more devoted to the Person and purpose of God and less focused on what He might do for us. As Tim Clinton writes:

> When we come to know God, we do so with the same selfish hang-ups we had prior to believing. But it's the Holy Spirit's working in our hearts and lives that ultimately removes the selfish motives and desires to move us toward a deeper relationship with him—one that is more focused on serving him, not ourselves.[1]

It is possible that our scars can become a road map for another person's healing. When Jesus showed Himself to His followers after the resurrection, He showed them His scars that were now being repurposed to demonstrate His love and grace. The Bible recounts a repurposing of the passion of Christ from fear and despair to joy.

> *So when it was evening on that day, the first day of the week, and when the doors were shut where the disciples were, for fear of the Jews, Jesus came and stood in their midst and said to them, "Peace be with you." And when He had said this, He showed them both His hands and His side. The disciples then rejoiced when they saw the Lord* (John 20:19-20).

Our repurposed scars draw us closer to God. Again Clinton writes:

God doesn't wipe away our past; instead, he uses every element of it—the wonderful, the horrible, and the senseless—to weave a new, beautiful, strong fabric of our lives. For the rest of our lives, we'll remember the events of the past, but they won't threaten us any longer. We'll be deeply grateful that God used them—even them—to teach us life's richest lessons and draw us closer to him.[2]

Revelation 21:5 says, *"Behold, I am making all things new."* When the word *behold* is used in the Scriptures, it generally means something new is about to be released. New vision. New depth of relationship with God.

In our ministry of formational counseling and spiritual direction, we have sought to bring people to an understanding of who they truly are in Christ. Part of that ministry is to help those to whom we minister to take inventory of all the steps that led up to their present season and show them that God can redeem and repurpose even the worst trauma. Whatever the issue, we have come to know that God is a repurposing God who turns trauma into triumph, failure into freedom, and pain into power.

Though our beloved friends found healing and peace, there often remained a question about what God might do with the debris field that lay behind them. How would someone who experienced a great loss or wounding possibly bring something positive out of their experience?

This repurposing, in fact, is part of the continuing unfolding of the artistry and presence of God in our lives.

God is a *repurposing* God who infuses new purpose in the artifacts of our journey resurrected from the sands of our wandering through our times of wilderness. Like the man with the house of repurposed building materials, our heaps of challenges and disappointments can become a habitation for the presence of God. What is needed is that we choose to see them as potential building materials for the Kingdom of God and release them to His feet for transformation and new purpose, where grief can become compassion for another's loss; where trauma and disappointment can bring new life; where a challenging diagnosis might become a new mission field—*"so that we will be able to comfort those who are in any affliction with the comfort with which we ourselves are comforted by God"* (2 Corinthians 1:4).

Let us now be open to seeing our lives with new eyes of hope and potential.

> *God can do anything, you know—far more than you could ever imagine or guess or request in your wildest dreams! He does it not by pushing us around but by working within us, his Spirit deeply and gently within us* (Ephesians 3:20 MSG).

TURNING ASIDE

Our journey is filled with transitions and broken pieces. Let's take time to inventory some of those broken pieces to see what the Great Artist and Craftsman of creation might do with them. In your own experience, what has God already repurposed in your life? This is an invitation to see what God sees.

Make a list of what comes to mind. We will watch to see how God might repurpose these to the benefit of His people, including you. Start your inventory with praise, reading and reflecting on the following verse:

> *You have turned my mourning into joyful dancing. You have taken away my clothes of mourning and clothed me with joy, that I might sing praises to you and not be silent. O Lord my God, I will give you thanks forever!* (Psalm 30:11-12 NLT)

NOTES

1. Tim Clinton, *God Attachment: Why You Believe, Act, and Feel the Way You Do About God* (New York, NY: Howard Books, 2010), 129.
2. Ibid., 163.

CHAPTER THREE

PICK-UP STICKS

Therefore, behold, I will allure her, and bring her into the wilderness, and speak to her heart (Hosea 2:14, author's translation).

A few years back I was sitting at my computer reflecting on the goodness of God and all of the blessings He had opened up in every realm of my life. My kids were doing well, and I was experiencing increased opportunities to speak into the lives of many hurting people, seeing them grow personally. God is good! In the middle of the voice of triumph, I opened a file to begin a new manuscript.

Just as the goodness of God was overwhelming and erupting from my heart, another voice began to vie for my attention from some deep and dark place. At first it was a faint thought, but the voice grew louder as I gave it space. This voice intruded into my peace, whispering, "Who do you think you are? You know the mess that's been in your life. Who do you think you are to minister to anyone or to write books about God. You are a mess, a flop, a failure. Who do you think you are!?"

I was caught off balance, flatfooted, and did not know what to do with the question. Then I asked myself, "Who do I think I am?" The words and the question were familiar to me. I have, at times, been a model of mediocrity and self-centeredness. Having allowed my heart to attend to these self-defeating thoughts, I simply deferred the question to the One who knows the answer: "Lord, who do *You* think I am?" Then a concert of silence. Nevertheless, the question continued, "Lord, who do *You* think I am?"

A little later while I was sitting in the lounge of a repair garage having my car serviced, I sensed the Lord saying, "I'm ready to answer your question now." The next moment brought an unexpected reply as my mind held an image of a child's game, Pick-Up Sticks. This image puzzled me as I hadn't thought about that game for many decades. How did this image of a kid's game answer my question? "Lord, who do You think I am?"

Pick-Up Sticks is played by dropping the bundle of brightly colored wooden or plastic "sticks" onto the floor or the top of a table resulting in what looks like a miniature, multicolored logjam, then moving the sticks one at a time from the pile using one black stick called the master stick. The score is calculated by the number and color of sticks moved without disturbing the other sticks. The sticks are moved using the master stick. I seldom played the game and was never very good at it when I did.

The more I thought about it, the clearer the meaning became. At times, my life, with all of its imperfections, reminds me of that little disheveled pile of sticks. The sticks are my many failings or challenges past and present, or maybe facets of my life that seem random and trivial. There are times when I hear God's invitation to greater intimacy or to join in what He may be doing; but instead of responding and moving ahead in God, I turn around and look at the little logjam behind me. I add up the score of the dropped sticks and consider myself the loser and disqualified. Then I'm stuck. I have to wonder how there could be any purpose in this pile of sticks—anything redeemable.

As I pondered the image of pick-up sticks, the Lord reminded me of another man with a few "sticks" in his life—Moses. Moses had an encounter with God on holy ground, a man who had received instruction from the personal presence of God. Eventually, Moses would lead thousands of God's people out of bondage, go through seemingly impossible obstacles, battle the enemies of God, and bring water out of a rock to a thirsty people. But before the power and glory, there was a wilderness.

THE WILDERNESS IS WILD

Now Moses was pasturing the flock of Jethro his father-in-law, the priest of Midian; and he led the flock to the west side of the wilderness and came to Horeb, the mountain of God (Exodus 3:1).

The key to our English word *wilderness* is *wild*. A wilderness is a wild or uncultivated place where we don't know the rules—where there is no map or GPS to get us around. There are many kinds of wilderness, from financial wilderness to cultural wilderness. We may find ourselves in a wilderness of a medical waiting room waiting to hear test results for ourselves or a loved one. Maybe we find ourselves in a wilderness of financial crisis or career loss. The wilderness can be growing older, sitting on the frontier of retirement. Grief can also be a wilderness. On grief, Alan Wolfet writes:

Think of your grief as a wilderness—a vast, mountainous, inhospitable forest. You are in the wilderness now. You are in the midst of unfamiliar and often brutal surroundings. You are cold and tired. Yet you must journey through this wilderness. To find your way out, you must become acquainted with its terrain and learn to follow the sometimes hard-to-find trail that leads to healing.[1]

Our personal wilderness seems to lack life or potential, causing us to give in to doubt or discouragement and feelings of being alone in the face of the formidable, unfamiliar, and untamed landscape before us.

BILL'S WILDERNESS

Bill was a man in his late middle age who had worked the same stable and predictable job for more than twenty years. The large company Bill worked for was shifting people into new positions to keep up with the changing times and technology. After his many years of service, Bill's supervisor informed him that he would be changing positions and roles within the organization. While Bill was assured that he would still have a good position within the company, he immediately felt uneasy. Change was not Bill's best friend. Change became Bill's wilderness and it caused him tremendous anxiety. He felt alone and unsure of what lay ahead.

The first day at his new position Bill crossed the threshold of a new building seeing unfamiliar faces and was led to a work station where he would perform a job he was not yet trained for. He experienced a panic attack and had to leave the facility. Bill was in a wilderness. Later, Bill was referred to our ministry for counseling in which we spent time looking at the source of his anxiety. As we prayed and talked, we found that his anxiety stemmed from an experience early in his life coming from a critical family and a particularly difficult time with a school teacher.

Bill was able to find truth and healing as he acknowledged his fear in the presence of the Lord and forgave the offenses that led to his anxiety. In effect, we had to reenter the wilderness of Bill's childhood and find God in the midst of it. Bill returned to work and engaged in his new position. In Bill's case, his wilderness required healing of an ungodly belief resulting in preparation for a whole new chapter of life.

There is a difference between a desert and the wilderness. Wilderness is a place or condition where there are still resources. You might think, for instance, of Jesus being in a place where He fed 5,000 and another 4,000 people as told in the Gospels. Our greatest resource in the wilderness is the Spirit of God. The wilderness, of whatever kind, can be unfamiliar and may seem lonely. However, the wilderness is also a season of listening to God, of separation and preparation. The Bible is filled with examples of individuals who experienced the wilderness, and God used that time to their benefit and to fulfill His purpose.

THE WILDERNESS IS A PLACE OF SEPARATION

I once heard a precious sister say, "I'm not sure where I'm going, but I'm sure I'll get there." In the wilderness, of whatever kind, the paths are unfamiliar. Most of the people who amounted to anything in the Bible of human existence went through times of wilderness. Consider Abraham, the friend of God. *"By faith Abraham, when he was called, obeyed by going out to a place which he was to receive for an inheritance; and he went out, not knowing where he was going"* (Hebrews 11:8).

To escape the pull and distractions of Ur, Abram had to leave the familiar. Genesis 12:1-3 tells us:

> *Now the Lord said to Abram, "Go forth from your country, and from your relatives and from your father's house, to the land which I will show you; and I will make you a great nation, and I will bless you, and make your name great; and so you shall be a blessing; and I will bless those who bless you, and the one who curses you I will curse. And in you all the families of the earth will be blessed."*

As with Abraham, our journey through times of wilderness relies on growing trust and connection with God.

A little while back I was serving a small church in northern Bedford County of Pennsylvania. I had driven the same route a couple of times each week to minister to this small group of precious people. One particular Sunday, after the morning service, I was driving home and decided to take a left instead of a right turn at a particular intersection. I thought I knew where the road would lead me. Some of the drive seemed familiar as I drove along a beautiful stream. But after half an hour or so, I realized I was totally lost. To make it more complicated, there was no cell service in this wild place so I could not call for direction nor find it with the GPS feature of my cellphone. I was adrift in a sea of trees and forest without a compass or stars to guide me.

I began to grip the steering wheel a bit more tightly as the territory, sprinkled with a few houses, looked less and less familiar. I recall saying something like, "God, I have no idea where I am." In a moment I seemed to hear the Lord say, "I know where you are. You are with Me." I loosened my grip and looked around at the scenery and enjoyed the rest of the drive. (It was only an hour longer than my usual drive.) I was not lost; God knew where I was. God knows where we are, in whatever kind of wilderness we may find ourselves.

There are varieties of wilderness, but whatever kind of wilderness we find ourselves in, of whatever description, it is a place of separation and preparation.

THE WILDERNESS IS A PLACE
OF QUIET AND LISTENING

The Jewish Publication Society translation of Exodus 3:1 reads, *"Moses went to the farthest end of the wilderness."* Wilderness separation is perhaps to the farthest side of the familiar. The wilderness may mean separation *from* what is familiar, but also separation *to* God. On one hand, our wilderness may be a place where we feel alone—but it can also be a place of an undistracted separation and solitude and a closeness to God.

The Gospels record Jesus seeking solitude in a wilderness to be alone with the Father more than forty times. Examples of His practice of solitude are found throughout the Gospels: *"But Jesus Himself would often slip away to the wilderness and pray"* (Luke 5:16). *"It was at this time that He went off to the mountain to pray, and He spent the whole night in prayer to God"* (Luke 6:12). (See also Luke 9:18; Matthew 14:23; John 6:15.) Jesus sought deliberate times of solitude with a greater emphasis on personal devotion to the presence of the Father. *The wilderness was a place of separation* to *God, not* from *Him.*

In that separation and solitude, we are changed. Speaking of the wilderness, Henri Nouwen wrote, "Solitude is the furnace of transformation. Without solitude we remain victims of our society and continue to be entangled in the illusions of the false self."[2] In the wilderness, we become who we truly are.

The wilderness is a place of separation to hear the voice of God. When Jesus was baptized as seen in the gospels, the voice of the Spirit declared, *"This is My beloved Son, in whom I am well-pleased"* (Matthew 3:17). But immediately, this same Spirit who announced His belovedness led Jesus into the wilderness:

> *Then Jesus was led up by the Spirit into the wilderness to be tempted by the devil. And after He had fasted forty days and forty nights, He then became hungry. And the tempter came and said to Him, "If You are the Son of God, command that these stones become bread." But He answered and said, "It is written, 'Man shall not live on bread alone, but on every word that proceeds out of the mouth of God'"* (Matthew 4:1-4).

The Hebrew word we translate as "wilderness" in the Hebrew Bible is *midbar,* which holds the word *dabar,* meaning "to speak." The Old Testament prophet Hosea records, *"Therefore, behold, I will allure her,* bring her into the wilderness and speak *kindly to her."* Jonathan Cahn writes, "So God brings us to the wilderness that we might hear His voice. Therefore, do not fear or despise the wildernesses of your life, and don't despise His removing of the distractions. Rather embrace it. Draw closer to Him."[3]

It may also seem true to us that God is silent in the wilderness. When God seems to be quiet, we must be even more quiet. The psalmist speaks the heart of God: *"Be still, and know that I am God"* (Psalm 46:10 NKJV).

The Wilderness Is a Place of Preparation

Most of the people who did great works for the Kingdom of God had times in the wilderness, so much so that we could fill an entire volume with those wilderness experiences. We have already mentioned Abraham who was told by God to leave all that was familiar to him to become a great nation.

Now consider Joseph who was thrown in a pit in the wilderness and sold into slavery by his brothers (see Genesis 37:22). Joseph endured the wilderness of slavery as the result of a false accusation by Potiphar's unfaithful wife, which landed him in prison. He endured the indignities of prison only to rise above his captivity to save his family and provide food for an entire nation in time of famine. Joseph became the salvation for his family and an entire nation (see Genesis 50:20).

There is a phrase repeated in the account of Joseph: *"The Lord was with Joseph"* (Genesis 39:2,21). The psalmist records the repurposing power of the wilderness, even the wilderness of unjust imprisonment:

> *He sent a man before them, Joseph, who was sold as a slave. They afflicted his feet with fetters, he himself was laid in irons; until the time that his word came to pass, the word of the Lord tested him. The king sent and released him, the ruler*

of peoples, and set him free. He made him lord
of his house and ruler over all his possessions
(Psalm 105:17-21).

In this wilderness Joseph was "tested," or perhaps it would be better to say that he was *refined.* Our times of wilderness remove all the dross of distraction while revealing the heart of God. In the wilderness, when we have exhausted our own reason and resources, the repurposing grace of God encompasses us. In a tender moment of reconciliation, Joseph speaks of God's repurposing grace saying, *"As for you, you meant evil against me,* but *God meant it for good in order to bring about this present result, to preserve many people alive"* (Genesis 50:20).

Also consider David, the overlooked or forgotten son of Jesse, who learned to defeat the enemies of his flock in the wilderness. In the simplicity and solitude of the wilderness, David became a *man after God's heart* (see 1 Samuel 13:14) who would decapitate a loudmouthed giant in the name of the Living God and would go on to become the great king of all the tribes of God's people.

Consider Jacob, the lying son of Isaac, who was sent off in fear and disgrace having stolen a blessing from his father, Isaac. Jacob would encounter God in the wilderness of Luz, wrestle with the angel of God, and then would become the father of the twelve tribes of Israel. God recounts the story of Israel in the Torah:

He found him in a desert land, and in the howl-
ing waste of a wilderness; He encircled him, He

cared for him, He guarded him as the pupil of His eye. Like an eagle that stirs up its nest, that hovers over its young, He spread His wings and caught them, He carried them on His pinions (Deuteronomy 32:10-11).

Consider what God did with Jacob in the wilderness from this passage in Deuteronomy 32. God *found* Jacob, *encircled* or *gathered* him into His arms, *cared* for him, *guarded* him, *hovered* over him, and *carried* him. Put yourself in the place of Jacob and the people of God. God, a carrying God, will do the same for you in the midst of whatever kind of wilderness you are in at this moment.

In the wilderness of whatever kind, the Lord removes us from the familiar, erases the blackboard, and perhaps even confuses our compass to speak to us in terms that defy our present understanding and that draw us closer to His heart. In our wilderness, God increases and we decrease as we depend solely on the presence and power of God moment by moment. In the wilderness, we are emptied so that we can be filled with God's presence and purpose.

The wilderness of whatever kind can also be a place of preparation to encounter God at a new depth. As we grow quieter, the Spirit of God leads us into something new or tender in His heart as we present ourselves to the Person and heart of God.

TURNING ASIDE

There are a few certainties about the wilderness: 1) you have been in one, 2) you are in one, or 3) you will be in one. Let's take some time to think about these three certainties. Consider past or present circumstances when you were in a wilderness of unfamiliarity. How did you connect with the heart of God in past times of wilderness? As you consider that time now, how was the Lord speaking to you in the wilderness? What did you carry out of that wilderness time?

You may be in a wilderness even as you read these words. You are not lost, beloved. The Shepherd knows where you are. He can find you and gather you into His arms. He cares for you; He is guarding you; His Spirit hovers over you even at this moment. Take time in a quiet place to read slowly through Deuteronomy 32:10-11, cited again below. Allow the Spirit to reveal the lost and wandering place in your life. Focus on the words I've bolded in the text. Spend a little time now breathing in those words and experiences. Use the spaces that follow to capture your personal responses to each of the bold words. Experience the truth of God's word.

> *He found him in a desert land, And in the howling waste of a wilderness; He encircled him, He cared for him, He guarded him as the pupil of His eye. Like an eagle that stirs up its nest, That hovers over its young, He spread His wings and caught them, He carried them on His pinions.*

Notes

1. Alan D. Wolfelt, *The Wilderness of Grief: Finding Your Way* (Buchanan, NY: Companion Press, 2010), 13.
2. Henri Nouwen, *The Way of the Heart: The Spirituality of the Desert Fathers and Mothers* (New York, NY: Harper Collins, 1981), 20.
3. Jonathan Cahn, *The Book of Mysteries* (Lake Mary, FL: Charisma House, 2018), 8.

Chapter Four

Repurposing of the Wilderness

Now Moses was pasturing the flock of Jethro his father-in-law, the priest of Midian; and he led the flock to the west side of the wilderness and came to Horeb, the mountain of God. The angel of the Lord appeared to him in a blazing fire from the midst of a bush; and he looked, and behold, the bush was burning with fire, yet the bush was not consumed. So Moses said, "I must turn aside now and see this marvelous sight, why the bush is not burned up." When the Lord saw that he turned aside to look, God called to him from the midst of the bush and said, "Moses, Moses!" And he said, "Here I am" (Exodus 3:1-4).

Put yourself in the sandals of Moses for a minute. Maybe you are in his sandals right now. What emotions and thoughts must have run through his heart and mind? Have you experienced similar emotions? This encounter on a mountain, often representing a place of solitude and reflection, at the edge of the wilderness, took place forty years after Moses fled from Egypt (see Acts 7:30). God had not forgotten Moses. Egypt was out of Moses' system, so to speak. Moses had gotten married, had a couple sons, and had nothing left but to shepherd the flocks of his father-in-law, Jethro.

What might Moses have thought as he sat alone at night by a campfire resting among the sheep? What thoughts might have been replayed in his head as he consumed some meager ration recalling the sumptuous foods of Egypt? I have to believe that as Moses listened to the bleating of sheep and the sound of the wind in the wilderness, there were remnants of disappointments and loss. But God has a long memory. He had not forgotten Moses.

Now as the embers of Moses' life and flight from Egypt were going out, a new flame was ignited in the form of a bush that burned but was not consumed. The far side of the wilderness brought Moses into a face-to-face encounter with the Eternal. The greatest rescue mission in the history of Israel began in this conversation. The man who likely believed his life was over was just beginning a new and powerful chapter. This conversation reveals a process that you and I go through to make sense of the pile of rubble in which we sometimes find ourselves.

One of the benefits of the wilderness and its silence is that it has the effect of preparing us to hear from God if we will turn aside from our own understanding to watch God transform our wilderness into a spring. As the psalmist says, *"He changes a wilderness into a pool of water and a dry land into springs of water"* (Psalm 107:35).

As you read these words, you are immersed in a sea of God's presence. Psalm 139:7 reads: *"Where can I go from Your Spirit? Or where can I flee from Your presence?"* The question is whether we are paying attention to the activity of God around us. Our times in the quiet of the wilderness prepare us for encounters with something new or unexpected, just as Moses encountered the Eternal in the form of a bush that burned, yet was not consumed. Moses was not, as far as we know from the text, a follower or seeker of Yahweh. But Yahweh is the Eternal Seeker. Jesus said, *"But an hour is coming, and now is, when the true worshipers will worship the Father in spirit and truth; for such people the Father seeks to be His worshipers"* (John 4:23).

In Exodus 3:2, most English translations cite that *"The angel of the Lord"* appeared to Moses. The Hebrew word here is *malach*, a messenger and manifestation of the presence of God. The word translated "Lord," *Yahweh*, literally means, "I am." Jesus Christ identified with the designation "I am" seven times in the Gospels:

- *"I am the bread of life"* (John 6:35).

- *"I am the Light of the world"* (John 8:12).

- *"I am the door"* (John 10:9).

- *"I am the good shepherd"* (John 10:11).

- *"I am the resurrection and the life"* (John 11:25).

- *"I am the way, and the truth, and the life"* (John 14:6).

- *"I am the vine"* (John 15:5).

In fact, when the guards came to arrest Jesus in the garden of Gethsemane, He deliberately referred to Himself as "I am" (see John 18:8). As I reflect on this passage, I believe the Messenger who appeared to Moses in his wilderness is none other than the pre-incarnate Jesus Christ, the Logos, the express image of the Father (see Colossians 1:15). Moses had a face-to-face, presence-to-Presence encounter with the Son of God.

There is a sequence to entering into this new season. Moses looked, then *turned aside* to see the presence of God. It is important to note that the presence of God was already aflame in the bush before Moses arrived on the scene. And so, God is at the edge of our own wilderness if we will open ourselves up to Him. Often, we are so mired in our wilderness of circumstance that we cannot lift up our eyes to see the presence of God. Our part in this sequence is to turn aside and look or watch for what God might be doing right in front of us.

To turn aside is to be willing to leave our regular path, opening ourselves to a new chapter in life. Turning aside involves moving in a new direction—finding new purpose and meaning even to the times we have spent in the wilderness. As we turn aside, God begins to repurpose our times of wilderness, trauma, disappointments. His presence is aflame before us as we open ourselves to new possibilities.

The Eternal God responded to Moses' *turning aside* as he presented himself to God. He had hit bottom and there was nothing left to hold on to. The clutter was gone. When the Lord saw that Moses turned aside to look, God *called* to him from the midst of the bush and said, "Moses, Moses!" So in the midst or at the edge of our wilderness of whatever kind, we see and turn aside, opening ourselves to the Presence of God, and God invites us to go a little further in our relationship with Him. We are cultivating a lifestyle of looking for God even in our times of challenge and unbinding the hand of God in our lives. We open to God; God opens to us.

Moses' response to the calling of God was a simple, *"Here I am"* (Exodus 3:4). This phrase, *"Here I am,"* is *hineniy* in Hebrew and is a presentation of ourselves to the very Presence and purpose of God. God called us to where we are. When He calls, He is not waiting for some more appropriate time or resolved circumstance; He calls in the middle of it. This simple phase, *"Here I am,"* is repeated throughout the Scriptures. When I read this phrase in the Scriptures, I'm expecting something new to be revealed in God. He is inviting us to His ways and His thoughts, which are higher than ours (see Isaiah 55:9).

Am I open? Am I available?

Jesus is the ultimate example of openness and availability to our Heavenly Father. One instance is a conversation Jesus had with a Samaritan woman at Jacob's well:

> *And He had to pass through Samaria. So He came to a city of Samaria called Sychar, near the parcel of ground that Jacob gave to his son Joseph; and Jacob's well was there. So Jesus, being wearied from His journey, was sitting thus by the well. It was about the sixth hour. There came a woman of Samaria to draw water. Jesus said to her, "Give Me a drink"* (John 4:4-7).

Here was Jesus, the only begotten Son of God, weary and thirsty at a well called Sychar, which was the same as Shechem in the Old Testament. Shechem was an important location representing a place of separation to God. It was at Shechem that God made a covenant of faith with Abraham (see Genesis 12). At Shechem Joseph was buried. At Shechem the Word of God was read and the covenant with Israel reiterated. Shechem is also between Mount Ebal and Gerizim. One represents the Kingdom of God, the other the world. Therefore, it was a place of separation to God and of decision. This was an encounter of thirst meeting thirst. Jesus went out of His way and His religion to speak with this non-Jewish woman to bring her water to quench an eternal thirst.

Another example of God's calling in the wilderness is Jesus in John 5 when He healed a man who had lain by the well at Bethesda for thirty-eight years. Of course, the religious establishment accused Jesus of coloring outside the lines and breaking the Sabbath, which, by the way, He never did. What is instructive to us is the statement that Jesus made to the religious folks: *"For this reason the Jews were persecuting Jesus, because He was doing these things on the Sabbath. But He answered them, 'My Father is working until now, and I Myself am working'"* (John 5:16-17). Jesus had to have walked by that location many times, yet on that day He was open to the Father to heal a hopeless man.

But we cannot fulfill the calling and invitation of God in our own strength and understanding.

> *Then He said, "Do not come near here; remove your sandals from your feet, for the place on which you are standing is holy ground." He said also, "I am the God of your father, the God of Abraham, the God of Isaac, and the God of Jacob." Then Moses hid his face, for he was afraid to look at God* (Exodus 3:5-6).

God has further instruction. Moses turned aside to see, then God called, and Moses responded, "Here I am." Now God says, in essence, "Take off your shoes, Moses." In other words, "Don't track the world and your understanding into My presence." The Kingdom of God is not

Burger King; you can't *have it your way*. In order for God to repurpose the wilderness, Moses had to relinquish all of his life to Him.

In this intimate encounter, Moses was unsure of himself as God called him into this great mission of deliverance. In that conversation, Moses responded to God's invitation with a question: *"Who am I?"* (Exodus 3:11). Then, when God sent Moses back to tell the people of God about his encounter with I AM, he asked God, "What if they don't believe me?" Whereupon God responded with the great repurposing question, *"What is in your hand?"* (Exodus 4:2). I can imagine a conversation that could have ensued here:

Moses says, *"What if…*they don't believe that You have *appeared* to me?"

God responds, "Moses, what is in your hand?"

Moses responds, "It's a stick, just a piece of dead wood."

I AM responds with another question, "Where did you get that stick, Moses?"

Moses, "Just back in the wilderness."

"Really. Well what do you do with that stick, Moses?

"I use it to protect myself from wild animals. Sometimes I use it as a tool…I mostly use it to lean on or carry it with me. It's just a stick—a piece of dead wood."

I can imagine God saying, "Moses, that stick which you see as just a piece of dead wood is all the disappointments you found in your wilderness. It's the pain, the loneliness, the hurts, the flops and failures. I'm going to *repurpose* it! Now cast that stick down at My feet. When you do, I am going to transform and empower it, and it will bring Me glory. With that stick in your hand, you will break the bonds of captivity. You will bring deliverance to the people from the power of false gods and take them through all kinds of obstacles, through the Red Sea, through hunger and thirst. You will be victorious in battles with the enemies to My Kingdom purposes. With your staff I hand you, you will bring living water out of the Rock. That stick in your hand will be the master stick!

"These sticks that I redeem and repurpose will be *the proof I've appeared to you.* That's who you are. That's why they will believe you, says I AM."

Beloved of God, the proof of our encounter with I AM is not our perfection; it's His repurposing of our sticks! If we will *turn aside* to see what He is doing and take off the sandals of our worldly understanding, He will call forth all our past hurts and challenges and repurpose them for His glory and the glory of His Kingdom. We must remove the shoes of our own understanding and operate in the truth of who He is. He is the I AM. The eternally creative and repurposing God. Those sticks in our life, when we present them to God, can be transformed and empowered as we lay them at His feet and make them our redemptive résumé.

In a larger sense, the cross of Christ is the master stick onto which the Master was affixed so cruelly. As the apostle Paul wrote, *"May it never be that I would boast, except in the cross of our Lord Jesus Christ, through which the world has been crucified to me, and I to the world"* (Galatians 6:14).

The sticks—the traumas, challenges and disappointments, and failures that you and I have carried for years that we may not have seen as valuable—can be presented at His feet, and He will redeem and repurpose them.

TURNING ASIDE

Let's take inventory. What are some of the sticks you have picked up in the wilderness? What did you learn—what compassion have they worked in your life? How might these sticks be repurposed if you placed them at the feet of I AM? What do you sense the Lord inviting you to place at His feet?

Part II

Life Repurposed

Honey in the Rock[1]

There's honey in the rock,

water in the stone,

Manna on the ground,

no matter where I go

I don't need to worry now

that I know (I know)

Everything I need You've got.

There's honey in the rock,

purpose in Your plan,

Power in the blood

Healing in Your hands

Started flowing when You said it is done

(Jesus). Jesus, who You are is enough.[2]

---

1   "Honey in the Rock," lyrics © Integrity's Praise! Music, Bethel Music Publishing, Maverick City Publishing Worldwide, Brandon Lake Music, A Wong Made Write Publishing, City And Vine Production Music, City And Vine Music Publishing International.

2   Author's note: It is suggested you listen to this song before reading the next chapters You Tube Link

Chapter Five

"Let My People Go!"

Then Moses said, "What if they will not believe me or listen to what I say? For they may say, 'The Lord has not appeared to you.'" The Lord said to him, "What is that in your hand?" And he said, "A staff." Then He said, "Throw it on the ground." So he threw it on the ground, and it became... [you complete the last sentence] (Exodus 4:1).

Here are a few focusing questions we might want to think about as we begin the repurposing process:

- How do we break free from the bondage of the past or present circumstance?
- How might our past or present challenges serve the purpose of God?

TRESA'S STORY

Tresa is a very gifted, very talented woman. She is a gifted artist and also a very gifted musician with a beautiful voice who plays guitar and writes inspirational songs. She performs locally in Central Pennsylvania and is an absolutely wonderful person. I've known her for many, many years. Tresa also works at a senior facility, helping the people there.

One day, Tresa was at work when she received a call from a family member who said, "You need to get to your sister's house quickly." Without hesitation, Tresa jumped in the car and, unsettled, drove to her sister Jaime's house. As she pulled up to the house, she was shocked to see the house surrounded by police cruisers and other official looking vehicles. *What could this be?* Jaime was Tresa's younger sister. Tresa has loved and cared for her as a mother would. In the same respect, when she saw the milieu of officials, like a mother her fears overwhelmed her for the well-being of her sister.

An officer approached Tresa and confirmed her worst fears. Her younger sister was attacked in her own home and had already passed away from her injuries. Tresa went into a shock and survival mode. She was held captive to grief and trauma, living under feelings of fear and anger toward God. She was frantic to make sure everybody was okay, even the family dog that she had found terrified and trembling against the garage door of a neighbor's house. (That dog is now part of Tresa's household.)

As we spent some period of time working through the various emotions that came upon her, there was a release and a greater peace. But the Lord had repurposing of her grief in mind. Tresa came to the place where she could see through the maze of her trauma. Trauma causes a facet of fear to block our view of life and constantly replay an internal video of horror that keeps us bound and hobbled. Our minds cannot sort through, cannot organize or have a frame of reference for something that's happened to us.

Tresa became afraid that something like what happened to her sister might happen to her. She then went to a place of wanting vengeance on the perpetrator. Then, also, there was the overwhelming shock associated with trauma, like trying to put ten pounds of potatoes in a five-pound bag. It just can't fit! There was also some survivor guilt because she had not communicated with her sister. Tresa was in a bondage of grief.

In order for us to heal, we need to deal with the inner monologue of our hearts. Our *sticks* have intruded upon our identity, growing like weeds around our hearts. They have become who we are. Our inner default says, "I'm the wounded person," or "I'm the offended person," or "I'm the person for whom it never works out right." Regardless, we carry our sticks into every facet of our lives. We may carry regrets. Perhaps we carry grief or disappointment. Worst of all, we miss the potential repurposing of our sticks. But the Lord has something greater for us.

There is a total release from this kind of bondage— bondage from the lies that bind us and prevent us from entering into our full purpose and destiny in God. Lies such as we are alone, we don't belong, we're not as good as, we're not good enough, we're not safe, we are ruined, we have no hope. Tresa found release as she encountered and debunked these lies in the presence of God. Her trauma was being repurposed.

After a few months and reconnecting with her grieving process, Tresa had the idea she would walk along with others who had experienced such family trauma. Tresa put up a Facebook page outreach to release others in grief. Her traumatic loss was becoming life for others. She went back to get further training as a grief counsellor and several people who now share in that community can process and heal with one another. She placed her loss at the feet of God, and He repurposed it to bring freedom to others.

The following are words to a song Tresa composed to express her love and grieving process. This was her expression of love and loss.

Where Love Is

I have seen darkness, but it's not who I am.
I've seen life taken before its time.
I always hoped that there
would be a better place,
I always believed that
love could save the day.
Evil repeats itself day after day,
It never makes anything all right.
Broken hearts are crying out in need,
"This is not where I want to be."
I want to live where love is.
I want to live in love.
I want to be where love is.
I want to live in love.
What if you and I could give up being right?
What if you and I could agree?
What if we meet in the
middle, no one has to win.
What if this disharmony could end?
I want to live where love is.
I want to live in love.
I want to be where love is.
I want to live in love.

We could summarize the deliverance of God's people from bondage in four questions that you found in the first few chapters of Exodus. In fact, the word

Exodus itself means a coming out of bondage. Here are the questions:

Moses asks, *"Who do you think I am?"* and *"How will they know You have appeared to me?"* (see Exodus 3:11; 4:1).

God asks, *"What is in your hand?"* (see Exodus 4:2).

Pharaoh asks, *"Who is Yahweh?"* (see Exodus 5:2).

Seven times Moses would command Pharaoh saying, "Let My people go," or as we said in an earlier chapter, "Send My people into the wilderness to worship Me." Pharaoh was about to learn the answer to his question, "Who is Yahweh?" This conversation was between Moses and Pharaoh, king of Egypt, who represents the power and the person of the devil.

Moses, the reluctant and stammering leader of Israel, was sent and commissioned to carry his stick into Pharaoh's throne room. As Moses carried his staff into the court of Pharaoh, a showdown was about to occur between light and darkness, good and evil. Yahweh had seen the bondage of His people and would loose them from the grip of slavery. See the following texts:

> *Therefore, say to the people of Israel: "I am the Lord. I will free you from your oppression and will rescue you from your slavery in Egypt. I will redeem you with a powerful arm and great acts of judgment. I will claim you as my own people, and I will be your God. Then you will know that I am the Lord your God who has freed you from your oppression in Egypt. I will bring*

you into the land I swore to give to Abraham, Isaac, and Jacob. I will give it to you as your very own possession. I am the Lord!" (Exodus 6:6-8 NLT)

So Moses and Aaron went to Pharaoh and did what the Lord had commanded them. Aaron threw down his staff before Pharaoh and his officials, and it became a serpent! Then Pharaoh called in his own wise men and sorcerers, and these Egyptian magicians did the same thing with their magic. They threw down their staffs, which also became serpents! But then Aaron's staff swallowed up their staffs. Pharaoh's heart, however, remained hard. He still refused to listen, just as the Lord had predicted (Exodus 7:10-13 NLT).

The power of the devil was swallowed up by the repurposing grace of God. As the narrative of freedom unfolded, Moses stick would bring down an entire pantheon of demonic influence. Each of the ten plagues represented a false and demonic god.

All these plagues were God's answer to Pharaoh's question: "Who is Yahweh?" and a direct assault on the power of the devil by the repurposing grace of God.[1] These emancipative plagues also are an answer to the question, "What is in your hand?" The repurposing grace of God swallows up and tears down the power of bondage and the wilderness.

As we *turn aside to see* what God might be up to, He will call forth and repurpose even the most difficult and dark circumstances to His glory. Tresa placed her grief at the feet of God, and the bleak winter of sorrow became a spring of new life for others in the bondage of trauma. In her wilderness, Tresa turned aside and responded to the calling of God. No power on Earth can overcome it. It's the most powerful force in the universe. The devil has no say over it. A pharaoh cannot hold us captive.

SET FREE FROM PHARAOH

God gave Moses three signs to show His power over Pharaoh. These three encounters demonstrated His repurposing grace to defeat the power of Pharaoh and release His people from bondage. The first sign was a serpent resembling the serpent on Pharaoh's headpiece. By this encounter with the serpent, God was stating that His power was far greater than Pharaoh's. The pharaohs of Egypt considered themselves to be gods. God was saying there is only one God—Yahweh! (See Exodus 4:3-4.)

The second sign was that of the leprous hand. Moses put his hand inside of his garment, and when he pulled it out, it was leprous. All types of skin diseases such as leprosy defiled a person from the presence of God. Yahweh was putting this earthly king in his proper place as a man showing he was not a God. (See Exodus 4:6-7.)

The third sign was turning the water into blood. That was a preview of the first plague that Moses called down, and again, all of these things happened with his staff in his hand. All of the plagues that were called down represented the ten false gods of Egypt. (See the table matching false gods with the various plagues.[1])

Nile to blood (Ex. 7:19)	Apis, the bull god, god of the Nile; Isis, goddess of the Nile; Khnum, ram god, guardian of the Nile
Frogs (Ex. 8:2)	Heqet, goddess of birth, with a frog head
Gnats (Ex. 8:16)	Set, god of the desert storms
Flies (Ex. 8:21)	Re, a sun god; Uatchit, possibly represented by the fly
Death of livestock (Ex. 9:3)	Hathor, goddess with a cow head; Apis, the bull god, symbol of fertility
Boils (Ex. 9:9)	Sekhmet, goddess with power over disease; Sunu, the pestilence god; Isis, healing goddess
Hail (Ex. 9:19)	Nut, the sky goddess; Osiris, god of the crops and fertility; Set, god of the desert storms
Locusts (Ex. 10:4)	Nut, the sky goddess; Osiris, god of the crops and fertility
Darkness (Ex. 10:21)	Re, the sun god; Horus, a sun god; Nut, a sky goddess; Hathor, a sky goddess

Death of firstborn (Ex. 11:5)	Min, god of reproduction; Heqet, goddess who attended women at childbirth; Isis, goddess who protected children; Pharaoh's firstborn son considered a god

Sometimes you and I have a false understanding or a false image of God. Do we see God as a compassionate God, or do we see ourselves as a victim of God? Our image and understanding of God needs to be healed. There is only one God and He is compassionate, gracious, merciful, and faithful (see Deuteronomy 34:5-7). Recall that Pharaoh's question was, "Who is Yahweh?" Through the signs provided for Moses and the subsequent plagues, God is demonstrating that He is that one God.

So how does this apply to you and me? We turn to false gods of prosperity or carnality. At best we pursue the false gods of religious practice absent the Presence of God. God's desire is constant with his people: "I will be their God, they will be My people, and I will live with them" (see Jeremiah 31:33).

NOTE

1. For full discussion of the plagues and their meaning see, *The Pharaohs, The Gods and The Plagues of Egypt* by Monica Dennis-Jones.

TURNING ASIDE

As you turn aside to the activity of God, what is He inviting you to place at His feet? Are there griefs? Disappointments? Challenges? Failures? How might God repurpose these?

Are there other false gods that you turn to in times of stress? What might they be? Renounce these gods and ask God to help you turn toward Him.

"Father, I need you in every way. I even need the strength of your Holy Spirit in order to turn aside toward you.

Set me firmly on your path and arrest me, Oh Lord. Help me turn aside from other gods and live face to face with You."

Chapter Six

In Over Our Heads

But Moses said to the people, "Do not fear! Stand by and see the salvation of the Lord which He will accomplish for you today; for the Egyptians whom you have seen today, you will never see them again forever. The Lord will fight for you while you keep silent" (Exodus 14:13-14).

FOCUSING QUESTIONS

- How does God respond when we are over our heads?

_____

_____

_____

_____

- How might God repurpose our overwhelming challenges?

_____

_____

_____

_____

How did you learn to swim? I have to say, I'm not much of a swimmer. However, I can remember how I learned to swim. When I was around 12 or 13 years old, I was with the Boy Scouts in a lake in the state of Indiana. I was in a canoe with a few other scouts and we paddled out to a small dock in water which was probably about 10 to 15 feet deep. Though I had previously had swimming lessons, I was somewhat afraid of water over my head, especially the murky waters of a lake. Suddenly, as I was standing on the dock, one of the other scouts pushed me into this murky water far over my head. So as we say, I was *in over my head*. Let's just say that I learned to swim very quickly.

Have you ever dived into murky waters where you can't see a foot in front your face? Think of the emotions that arise when we are in over our heads, when we're fighting for breath. It reminds me of the scripture above and the 14th chapter of Exodus. The Israelites had Pharaoh and his army *behind them* and the Red Sea *before them*. If we look at the context carefully, we learn that the Israelites were accusing Moses of something like genocide by bringing them out of captivity. Now they were captive to fear at this seemingly insurmountable obstacle before them and certain annihilation creeping up on them.

How does God respond when we're in over our heads? He is our spiritual lifeguard! All of us have fallen or been pushed into certain circumstances where we are over our heads. I, like the reluctant swimmer, flailed through the water frantically trying to preserve my life. We might be over our heads in our finances or perhaps some past failure or present challenge or sin or trying to break free from self-condemning thoughts. When we are in over our heads, the Lord doesn't just throw us a life preserver. Christ, the Son of God, walks on the murky water. It's not over His head!

So just as Pharaoh's army was hard on the heels of the Israelites, we also have issues behind that can be repurposed. And just as the Red Sea was before them, there are some obstacles that we feel are insurmountable.

What does God do in those cases? How does God apply His repurposing grace to these situations past, present, or future?

> *Behold, O Lord, You know it all. You have enclosed me behind* [past] *and before* [future], *And laid Your hand upon me* [present] (Psalm 139:4-5).

> *Then the Lord said to Moses, "Why are you crying out to Me? Tell the sons of Israel to go forward. As for you, lift up your staff and stretch out your hand over the sea and divide it, and the sons of Israel shall go through the midst of the sea on dry land. As for Me, behold, I will harden the hearts of the Egyptians so that they will go in after them; and I will be honored through Pharaoh and all his army, through his chariots and his horsemen. Then the Egyptians will know that I am the Lord, when I am honored through Pharaoh, through his chariots and his horsemen"* (Exodus 14:15-18).

This is where imagination meets the impossible—the imagination of God. Who would have imagined that it would be possible to divide a sea and bait Pharaoh with a mob of former slaves? It's the same imagination that conceives a bush that burns but is not consumed. When confronted with the impossible, we are standing on holy ground. On holy ground we take off our shoes and don't track our understanding into the presence of God.

God can do anything, you know—far more than you could ever imagine or guess or request in your wildest dreams! He does it not by pushing us around but by working within us, his Spirit deeply and gently within us (Ephesians 3:20 MSG).

THE GOD OF TIGHT PLACES

God is our refuge and strength, a very present help in trouble (Psalm 46:1).

It was every parent's worst nightmare. I got the call as I was beginning a ministry session at about 10 in the morning. I was told that our youngest daughter, Christina, had been in an accident, but that she was OK. She had some kind of injury and was being taken to the local hospital emergency room. I left the appointment with apologies and drove the short distance to the hospital, where I was joined in a few minutes by my wife, Carol. She was the one who had been called first after the accident by someone at the scene. In fact, our daughter herself had talked to her mother over the cell phone, though Christina was very confused about what had happened.

Carol and I, like most parents, had to wait. We stood in the driveway of the emergency entrance, waiting for an ambulance to arrive, but it never arrived! We strained to see each time an ambulance arrived, always wondering if Christina was on board and expecting to hear her saying something like, "This is no big deal!" Christina was our youngest—our baby. She was and is an impressive young woman with a desire to help and heal people in the community. As we waited, it became apparent that Christina was not going to be coming there after all. We went inside the emergency waiting room and asked what they knew. All they could tell us was that they were not going to be receiving anyone from the accident because two of the three people had been life-lined by helicopter to the trauma unit at the Hershey Medical Center and that one person had died at the scene of the accident.

The very words "trauma unit" shook us to the core. Eventually I was given the number of the local state police station, and an understanding trooper told us that indeed Christina was one of those who had been airlifted to the trauma unit in Hershey. When we told them who we were at Hershey Medical Center, we were put on hold until our call was transferred to the hospital chaplain. He, like the others, was unable to tell us anything about Christina's condition other than the fact that he had talked to her and that the doctors were hard at work on her. So Carol and I drove the one-and-a-half-hour drive to Hershey, which seemed like eight hours to us, for we were in a state of shock and total ignorance about our daughter's condition. I wish I could say that our hearts were encouraged by the fact that the Lord was in control and that everything would work out for good. However, I did not feel those assurances as we headed north on Interstate 81. I was afraid and could hardly hold myself together.

As we drove to the hospital, many flashbacks replayed in my mind of times when our little one had been hurt or traumatized in various ways. I remembered other times when I felt helpless as a parent—the times when, as a father, I felt there was nothing I could do to help my kids. But at no time in my life or hers did I feel as helpless and weak as I did on this day. My faith was wavering and my mind was wondering, "God, how could You allow this to happen to our child? How? Why?" Both words we throw out before God when we are in over our heads. This was overwhelming to me, and my impulse was to weep, but someone had to be the dad, and I figured it had to be me, though I felt more like a helpless little boy than a father. All Carol and I could do was to pray, "Lord, have mercy on our daughter." When we arrived at Hershey, we were taken to a little room adjacent to the trauma wing. In a few minutes a delightful man, Chaplain Herb, met us and prayed with us. He could not tell us anything about Christina, but waited with us until one of the many doctors who were attending our "baby" could come and talk to us.

Eventually, the doctor came in and began to describe what seemed like an incredible array of injuries that Christina had suffered. We were taken to the unit and were greeted by the sights and sounds of medical high technology. We walked into the room through a sliding glass panel and caught sight of our daughter who was lying in a bed surrounded by lights and beeps and gauges indicating the various functions of her physical being. I walked around to the left side of the bed and caught sight of our bruised and bloody girl; she had a respirator tube down her throat, her hair was matted with blood, and there was a long, sutured cut on her pretty forehead. Then, as I looked at her, I spoke her name. Her left eyelid rose, revealing one of those big brown eyes of hers. Though her body was battered, I knew there was still a Christina alive and unaltered in there somewhere.

At that point I did not know what to say to our daughter. I knew she was experiencing pain beyond my imagination. I wish I could say that the Spirit of God rose up in me and that I uttered great and faithful prayers. However, I could not pray; I was paralyzed and weak. The mother of Christina's boyfriend came into the room and stood by her. She asked me, "Did you pray for Christina?" I could not even muster a response, as my eyes welled up with tears. I could not pray or say a word. All I could do was look at the various machinations of high-tech medicine and wonder to myself how we would be able to get through this challenging time. Both Christina and her parents seemed to be in over our heads. I was especially focused on myself, feeling sorry and sad. Christina had to go through something like 16 hours of surgery over the next few days. We pretty much lived in the trauma center waiting room. I met a few interesting folk who were going through some of the same kinds of pain we were experiencing. Our family was *in over our heads*.

How in creation could God bring anything good out of this? It was and is beyond human imagination. In principle this may have held similar emotions such as Moses and Israel felt when facing the Red Sea. They had slavery in Egypt behind them and fathoms of hopelessness before them.

To understand the repurposing of this event we have to go back to the beginning context of the situation. Summarizing a few verses here, we can find a similar pattern to that which Moses followed.

S.T.O.P.

- See: God led them at the edge of wilderness to the place where He alone might rescue them (see Exodus 13:20).

- Turn aside: Moses turned off his normal path to see what God was up to (see Exodus 13:18).

- Open to God's Purpose and power: "the wind or the Spirit of God" that made a highway through the impassable obstacle before them making a way for Israel to cross over on dry ground (see Exodus 14:21).

- Present to God's grace: Israel saw God's great power over their past captures (see Exodus 31).

So then, how did the Lord re-purpose Moses' life to bring about God's purpose? Moses was raised in the house of Pharaoh with all the royal benefits such as education and leadership. Subsequent to that, he spent many years in the wilderness of his own. That wilderness brought Moses to the end of himself. Moses had all of the training in body, mind, and particularly attitude to lead perhaps hundreds of thousands of people out of bondage and then to promise. Our times in the wilderness tend to have a humbling effect on us as we learn to depend upon God more than ourselves. *"Now the man Moses was very humble, more than any man who was on the face of the earth"* (Numbers 12:3). The exodus of the people of Israel follows a similar pattern that Moses had when he encountered God at the burning bush.

So how does this apply to you and me when we are faced with challenge? We must do what Moses did: turn aside and open ourselves to God's purpose and imagination. We See the activity of God, we Turn aside from our path, we Open ourselves to God by removing the shoes of our own understanding, and then Present our stick to God on holy ground (S.T.O.P.). The most important thing is to get quiet and consider what possibilities there might be in God. He has purpose in whatever situation. Let me share the rest of our story with Christina.

In order to get some closure regarding Christina's accident, I drove to the wrecking yard where they had towed her car after the accident and asked to see it. They knew immediately which car it was and led me to it. I could see some look of concern and perhaps compassion on the faces of the guys in the shop as I walked around to the place where the car was stored. I saw only the back end of the car at first. When I came around to the front of the car I was amazed. The front of her car and the passenger compartment were crushed and compressed into a tiny space. How could she have survived this impact? The airbag had been deployed, and it looked as if the steering wheel was bent over from the impact of her upper body. How did she not get crushed? As the fears of what might have been began to crowd into my mind, an odd peace began to settle within me. I heard God speaking these words to my heart: "I am abundantly available in tight places." It was an interpretation of Psalm 46:1 that I had preached on a few years before.

> God is our refuge and strength, a very present help in trouble. Therefore we will not fear, though the earth should change and though the mountains slip into the heart of the sea; though its waters roar and foam, though the mountains quake at its swelling pride. ... The Lord of hosts is with us; the God of Jacob is our stronghold (Psalm 46:1-3,7).

My interpretation of this scripture came from the notes in the margins of my Bible. According to the margin notes of the New American Standard Updated translation, the Hebrew of the text could be simply and literally interpreted as "*God was abundantly available in tight places.*" I looked again at the car and saw that it was indeed a tight place. God was telling me that He had been there in that tight place with Christina and in fact had been with her in every tight place she had ever experienced.

We have a tendency to see the presence of God as some kind of mysterious and impersonal force, like something out of Star Wars. But this was not some mysterious force that was with her, but the very person of Christ who was full of compassion for Christina. As the Lord continued to speak to my heart, I could see Him in and around that crunched car in so many ways. I envisioned Him sitting beside Christina immediately before the crash and at the moment of impact. It was as though His hand had slipped between her and that airbag. Then I remembered that one of Christina's friends, with whom she had gone through most of her junior high and high school years, was driving by within a minute or so of the accident and saw the aftermath of the wreck. The Lord told her to pull over and help, as she had some medical training. She heard a voice from the car asking for someone to call Carol, her mother. Christina's friend stayed with her the whole time, praying with her and trying to stop the bleeding from an injury on her head. Her friend Larissa was the present help, the abundant availability of God, for that moment.

In addition to Larissa, a nurse who had been traveling behind Christina had a cell phone with which to call Carol. It was the comforting hand of God already beginning to assure us of His care, though at the time we did not hear Him through the din of trauma and worry. Next the vision switched to the EMTs on the scene. They were the hand of God all over Christina as she was flown to a place of help by the life-line flight. It was a place that had been prepared by the love and compassion of God. When Christina arrived at the trauma unit, as many as ten people worked on her at one time. There were plastic surgeons, neurosurgeons, orthopedic surgeons, and many other technicians. Though all of this looked like a high-tech medical wonder, it was in fact the "very present help" of God in that tight place. Chaplain Herb was the still, small voice of God speaking to us about the hospital after her birth. I now saw her cradled in the arms of one of the OB staff. (By the way, she was born at Hershey Medical Center as well.) When she was burned as a toddler, it was a kindly older doctor who ministered to her little face and hand so calmly and gently. On and on it went until I was finally able to see the Person of the Lord involved in every stage of her life and ours.

Many of us have accused God of apathy based solely on circumstantial evidence. We believe when we catch a cold or develop cancer that somehow God is disinterested in us, that He does not love us. We fail to see the faithfulness of God. The reality is that we live in a world that is filled with colds, cancers, and crashes as a result of the fall. These things are not God's fault, nor are they His plan. They are just life.

The Lord is faithful to us in the midst of the inevitable trials we face. He did not tell us that we would never face trials, but that He we would be with us in trouble. He said, *"I will be with him in trouble; I will rescue him and honor him. 'With a long life I will satisfy him and let him see My salvation'"* (Psalm 91:15-16). To see His salvation is to see Him in the midst of the difficulty. The word *salvation* and the name of Jesus come from the same root. Jesus is the Person of God in the world of people. He is the fullness of God's mercy and faithfulness. But the plan of God does not end there. If we will See, Turn, Open, and Present ourselves to Him, He will repurpose our encounter and sticks for His purpose and glory.

Again, God promised that He would be with us in the fire. He promised:

> *When you pass through the waters, I will be with you; and through the rivers, they will not overflow you. When you walk through the fire, you will not be scorched, nor will the flame burn you. For I am the Lord your God* (Isaiah 43:2-3).

Christina is now married and a mother. Now, a few years after the accident, I was sitting at a local restaurant with Christina and her little girl, Hannah. I looked across the table at Christina's face and noticed that there was a barely visible scar on her forehead. As I looked at this reminder of God's favor, I was moved to tears (not a rare thing in my life these days). As we were leaving one another's company, I leaned over and kissed this little scar on her pretty forehead, though I did not make a big deal of it. This scar was a reminder of God's faithful and merciful intervention—the manifestation of His goodness to our family. I kiss the scars of Jesus' wounds as well as they too are reminders of His faithfulness. Now that I have seen the faithful hand of God at work in each of these circumstances, I am *"fully persuaded that, what he had promised, he was able also to perform"* (Romans 4:21 KJV). He is "abundantly available for help in tight places." The tighter the place, the more abundant He becomes. *"Therefore we will not fear, though the earth should change and though the mountains slip into the heart of the sea"* (Psalm 46:2).

God repurposed the trauma in that while Christina was in the hospital she encountered several social workers. She was already a psychology major, but this encounter with the real social workers ultimately culminated in a doctorate. She is now an assistant professor of social work equipping others to carry people through the *tight places* of real life.

Sometimes in our life we have major events that seem to divide the past from the present—like Christina's accident for us. But just the routines of our life can be punctuated day by day by one wilderness or another.

CAROL'S RECOLLECTIONS OF GOD'S REPURPOSING GRACE

In our introduction, Thom mentioned his illness. For at least three or four months before I took him to the hospital, we went from one doctor to another, from one specialist to another. The progression of his physical body spiraling downward was more than alarming, and I felt helpless to stop it. For weeks before that major event when he stopped breathing in the hospital, he was coma-like and unavailable. This was all happening during the really dark part of COVID when hospitals were closed to visitors, even relatives—even wives. Our friends were beside me; our social worker daughter was searching out a hospital where a close relative and advocate would be permitted; and Amy, our oldest daughter, believe it or not, is an experienced nurse. I saw these children of ours in a new way—they had grown up and were competent young women not only at home, but in their professions and as caring adults. In them was grace upon grace, miracle upon miracle, and provision upon provision. Every day as I talked to doctors, although I was the only one allowed to be there beside my husband, Amy was on the phone in my hand on facetime talking and advocating, directing, intervening for her father. I did not have to be overwhelmed by complicated medical decisions and the milieu of medical terms and technology. Amy would turn to me and explain the immediate situation and my best options and her advice. Her experience was broad, even to the point of working in an ER for five years. I won't bore you with all the details, but today with the help of our friends and these incredible people that I didn't even realize were living inside my children, we experienced the repurposing grace of God. We sold our home in a day and bought the perfect home Amy had found for us closer to her.

The truth is, we will not get younger, we will have medical concerns, there will be shaky times. When I look back, I still wonder how I sat in an attorney's office attending to our wills while my husband was in a coma—except that beside me sat Thom's niece. How did this lovely new house that my daughter prayed about for us, "Please Lord, the only present I want for my birthday is for my parents to have this house," how did the present contract on that house fall through and become available to us on her—yes—on her birthday? I could go on about all the kindness and goodness the Lord brought to us. But here is the point: had I not stopped and turned aside (I really believe God arrested me because I am like a train sometimes), I would have missed them all—all the times that the Lord put people around me to hold up my arms and all the times the Lord showed us His faithfulness, His goodness, and His grace.

Now, Thom and I are more unified. Even now, I chuckle when I think that this book was started three years ago before I became part of it! Before his illness, I was teaching and he was writing. Now, three years later as we finally finish this book, our lives are more inter-twined because together we have walked through a Red Sea. Every day we are aware of the grace that abounds in the unity and oneness that we experience as we help one another and work together, write together, pray together, and yes, work through a myriad of residual effects of such a debilitating illness, and together embrace the goodness of God.

As we reflect upon this account of Israel at the Red Sea and our daughters and their husbands, their families and children, and our friends, when we look back upon a lifetime of grace that God has poured out on us, the text of Miriam's song of victory and praise comes to mind.

> *I will sing to the Lord, for He is highly exalted; the horse and its rider He has hurled into the sea. The Lord is my strength and song, and He has become my salvation; this is my God, and I will praise Him; my father's God, and I will extol Him. The Lord is a warrior; the Lord is His name* (Exodus 15:2-4).

TURNING ASIDE

This moment, as you read this chapter, you may have a pharaoh behind you and a Red Sea before you.

These can seem overwhelming. But God has repurposing grace for you.

See: Take a few minutes to think about and write down those things behind you in the past that hold you captive. It won't be difficult as you carry them with you all the time. This is the time to put them to rest.

Turn: Bring yourself to a quiet focus to the presence of God. You may do this by simply repeating the phase, *"You are the God of tight places."*

Open: Listen in the quiet place as the Lord brings new possibilities to mind. How might the Lord repurpose your sticks?

Present: Are you willing to remove your shoes—your own understanding and interpretation of circumstances past, present, and future? It is in the times of wilderness that we hear and grow in God and learn who He is. Jesus asked His disciples, "Look, who do you say that I am?" Peter stood up and said, "You are the Messiah. You're the Son of God," and Jesus said, "Flesh and blood didn't reveal this to you, My Father in heaven told you this" (see Matthew 16:16).

Make your wilderness a place of worship, beloved. Allow your repurposed stick to swallow up the lies that hold you captive.

As we cast our sticks at the feet of Yahweh, He brings us out of bondage. Remember the question that Pharaoh asked was, "Who is Yahweh?" How does your life answer this question?

Pray this with me:

> *Lord Jesus, I choose today to stop my current course of focusing on my circumstance. I choose to turn aside from my own way and to open my heart to You and to present my sticks to You.*

Chapter Seven

Water from the Rock

Then all the congregation of the sons of Israel journeyed by stages from the wilderness of Sin, according to the command of the Lord, and camped at Rephidim, and there was no water for the people to drink. Therefore the people quarreled with Moses and said, "Give us water that we may drink." And Moses said to them, "Why do you quarrel with me? Why do you test the Lord?" But the people thirsted there for water; and they grumbled against Moses and said, "Why, now, have you brought us up from Egypt, to kill us and our children and our livestock with thirst?" So Moses cried out to the Lord, saying, "What shall I do to this people? A little more and they will stone me." Then the Lord said to Moses, "Pass before the people and take with you some of the elders of Israel; and take in your hand your staff with which you struck the Nile, and go. Behold, I will stand before you there on the rock at Horeb; and you shall strike the rock, and water will come out of it, that the people may drink." And Moses did so in the sight of the elders of Israel. He named the place Massah and Meribah because of the quarrel of the sons of Israel, and because they tested the Lord, saying, "Is the Lord among us, or not?" (Exodus 17:1-7)

Here are a couple of focusing questions for this chapter:

1. What is our true thirst?

2. How does water from the Rock point to Jesus Christ?

Have you ever been thirsty? I mean really thirsty, like your tongue sticking to the roof of your mouth thirsty. I recall during my years in college that in the summertime I worked to build fences. Most of those days were very hot and hard. We might be working out in the middle of nowhere with no shade under the hot sun. Often, we would construct 100 to 200 feet of fence in a day, mostly in the hot sun. A few times I almost passed out from thirst with profuse sweating. I recall one day we were building a backstop at the local baseball park. It must have been 95 to 100 degrees that day out in the open, no shade whatsoever. I recall that I must have drunk two gallons of water that day. I was weary, worn out, and ready to fall over. To say the least, I was thirsty.

THIRST MEETS THIRST

Jesus answered and said to her, "If you knew the gift of God, and who it is who says to you, 'Give Me a drink,' you would have asked Him, and He would have given you living water. …Everyone who drinks of this water will thirst again; but whoever drinks of the water that I will give him shall never thirst; but the water that I will give him will become in him a well of water springing up to eternal life" (John 4:10,13-14).

As we read the preceding verses, we can clearly see that Jesus and the woman He met at the well in Sychar were both thirsty. We might take note in the previous verses that the woman stated the well was very deep. We all have a deep thirst. I've seen a painting of these verses in which the woman was surrounded by a very long rope. Perhaps the rope could represent the long journey trying to fulfill that thirst. Beloved, I know the only way our deep spiritual thirst is going to be satisfied is if we fully embrace Christ. I know also that He has a thirst to be with us, and we are trying to satisfy that thirst with myriads of different kinds of things—possessions, positions, potions, etc. Thirst must meet thirst!

I wonder if this thirst was something like what the children of Israel experienced as they launched into the wilderness. Imagine with me, if you will, a very large group of people who were fleeing a murderous army and had just escaped certain death by going through the impassable obstacle of the Red Sea. Now they were entering into a place of wilderness, becoming very thirsty, and what did they find? A rock!

The Bible is filled with stories of thirsty people, from the children of Israel to the woman at the well to John 7:37, *"If anyone is thirsty, let him come to Me and drink."* When we are truly, deeply thirsty, we will do almost anything to satisfy our thirst. I think of the song that says, "As the deer pants (or longs) for the water, so my soul longs for you." I remember my dad often said we could not get blood out of a turnip. True. But this picture of thirsty people in front of a rock seems even more impossible. This image of the rock in Scripture is a foreshadowing of Jesus Christ. In Exodus 16–17, the Lord satisfies the deep thirst of His people and even more. If we search the entire body of Scripture, we find that Jesus was not only water from the Rock, He was the Bread of Life, and Honey from the Rock as well.

> *And I have come down to deliver them out of the hand of the Egyptians and to bring them up out of the land to a good and broad land, a land flowing with milk and honey, to the place of the Canaanites, the Hittites, the Amorites,*

the Perizzites, the Hivites, and the Jebusites. (Ex.3:8, ESV) (See also Deut. 32:13 and Psalm 81:1) Water is one of those mega themes throughout Scripture, from the four rivers that flow out of the Garden of Eden to some of the words of Jesus from the cross to the Stream that flows through the New Jerusalem in Revelation. In the wilderness, water is the difference between life and death. As water is the difference between natural life and death, Jesus is the difference between spiritual life and death supplying all we need—the Bread of Life, the Water of the Spirit, the Abundant Life.

IN MOSES	IN CHRIST
	Bread of Life
Then the Lord said to Moses, "Behold, I will rain bread from heaven for you; and the people shall go out and gather a day's portion every day, that I may test them, whether or not they will walk in My instruction" **(Exodus 16:4)**.	*Jesus said to them, "I am the bread of life; he who comes to Me will not hunger, and he who believes in Me will never thirst"* **(John 6:35)**.

IN MOSES	IN CHRIST
	Spirit
Then the Lord said to Moses, "Pass before the people and take with you some of the elders of Israel; and take in your hand your staff with which you struck the Nile, and go. Behold, I will stand before you there on the rock at Horeb; and you shall strike the rock, and water will come out of it, that the people may drink." And Moses did so in the sight of the elders of Israel **(Exodus 17:5-6)**.	Now on the last day, the great day of the feast, Jesus stood and cried out, saying, "If anyone is thirsty, let him come to Me and drink" **(John 7:37)**. Let the one who believes in me drink. Just as the scripture says, "From within him will flow rivers of living water" **(John 7:38 NET)**.
	Abundant Life
But I would feed you with the finest of the wheat, and with honey from the rock I would satisfy you **(Psalm 81:16)**.	The thief comes only to steal and kill and destroy; I came that they may have life, and have it abundantly **(John 10:10)**.

BETWEEN A ROCK AND A HARD PLACE

What do we think of when we see the image of a rock or stone? I tend to think of a rock as something hard or impassable. We all face some sort of a difficult place at times, which brings to mind the saying *between a rock and a hard place.* That saying has its origin in Greek mythology when Odysseus had to pass between a cliff in a whirlpool. The whirlpool seems like it can suck us down and under the waves. The cliff is inhabited by a man-eating monster, something to consume us. To call for water to flow from a rock would be like expecting a bird to swim or a fish to fly.

We all might be traversing this kind of path at times. But as we *turn aside* and *present* ourselves to God, He will call forth those sticks we've carried with us to bring about His purposes, not in spite of our challenges and disappointments but because of them. Looking at the scripture above, in Exodus God would have us "strike that Rock" with our staff in our hands. In plain English, we must apply the *repurposing grace of God* to somehow bring Christ into the midst of our situation. We See that God may be doing something right in front of us; we Turn aside to see what He is doing; we Open ourselves to His Presence and purpose; and we Present ourselves to Him. At the risk of being redundant, S.T.O.P.

I recently met a man who we might have said was stuck between a rock and a hard place. He was a man who had experienced his own time of wilderness via several years of incarceration. But God spoke to this man revealing a new pathway for him and for countless others as he placed that stick, that challenge and disappointment, at the feet of Yahweh. And that stick is now being transformed to bring water, life, and abundance out of the Rock that is Christ.

For I do not want you to be unaware, brethren, that our fathers were all under the cloud and all passed through the sea; and all were baptized into Moses in the cloud and in the sea; and all ate the same spiritual food; and all drank the same spiritual drink, for they were drinking from a spiritual rock which followed them; and the rock was Christ (1 Corinthians 10:1-4).

TORRIANO'S STORY IN HIS OWN WORDS

I remember standing in the courtroom and the judge asking me to tell him what happened for me to arrive in his courtroom, and to begin at the absolute beginning. At that point I was wondering, "Well, what is the beginning? What is beginning that led me to be in this courtroom facing charges of aggravated murder, attempted murder, and felonious assault?" The beginning is just a series of lives impacting one another that allowed me to be in this courtroom, one of whom was my grandmother.

My grandmother came of age in the 1920s-30s, which was a terrible time for African American people, even worse for African American women. She was married at a very young age to a much older man who was terribly abusive. My grandmother in turn was a strong disciplinarian. She raised my mother, my aunts, and my uncles with a firm hand believing that her children would not have to rely on anyone like she had to rely on her husband, and so she wasn't very affectionate. Her idea of demonstration of love was her preparing you for a cruel, unforgiving world. My mother used to tell my sister and me that she didn't have a good relationship with our grandmother. She said, "I don't even want to be your mother. I want to be your friend." And that's what we became. We became friends.

My father and my mother got divorced at a very young age, so I never knew my father. Only talked to him once in my entire life. In my childhood I was living in Cleveland, Ohio with a single mom who struggled with drugs and alcohol and who didn't spend time with my sister and me. I began to use drugs and alcohol at a very young age—12, 13, 14 years old—to cope with a lonely life. It was a very lonely time.

And I remember that inside of my chest, I couldn't understand, express, really articulate exactly what I was feeling, but I had this desire for the love of a father that I never knew. The closest I came to that was an uncle— DP. He was an incredible man. He became a father figure to me, secure and impressive. But he was snatched out of my life early, too early, for which I blamed God. And that's really when my life took a downward trajectory, a downward turn.

Soon I started running with the gangs in my local neighborhood. This was the first time that I felt a sense of belonging. It seemed to fill a void inside of me. And so, I grew up stealing, robbing, and doing drugs and alcohol. At this time, I was sent from home to home, from juvenile detention facility to the next. From one foster home to a group home, from one family member's home to another family member's home. Life was totally chaotic. Both my sister and mother were alcoholics and drug addicted. But God had a plan!

One day my mother came home and she just had this radical news, and she informed us that she had in fact given her life to Jesus Christ and that she would no longer be the same. We laughed at her. It became a lot more serious as she began to walk around the house and pray for us and try to touch us and invite us to go to church. This made me mad. I told my mother not to talk to me about *her* Jesus. I blamed my mother for everything: drugs, alcohol, for divorcing my father. I didn't want to hear anything from her or her Jesus. But she prayed anyway.

One night I went out looking to get high and found a guy who sold drugs and robbed him of his drugs and his money. He had access to a gun, and he got that gun and while I was fleeing, he was shooting at me. I narrowly got away. I ran to my mother's house; this woman had been praying for me. And I had a moment of clarity. I realized in this moment that maybe there is something more to this life, maybe. And so, I said, "Hey, I'll give it a try." So I stopped using drugs, stopped drinking. Even stopped smoking cigarettes. And this was for about a week or two, and I was feeling great, and I didn't really know what to do with my new life.

Sometime later I went out for a walk after dinner. As I was standing in the park I heard this voice: "Hey man, do you remember me?" I turned around and I saw this guy (whom I had robbed) and said, "Nah, I don't remember you." But when he took his hat off, I remembered him distinctly. It was the guy I had robbed a couple of weeks earlier. He said, "Yeah, I got you now." And he pulled out a gun, and staring down the barrel of that gun, I knew that my life was over. My life and the life of my mother and all the others I had known passed before me, and in the stillness of that moment, I realized that my life is not my own.

Before I knew it, someone jumped between me and the guy with the gun and said, "No, don't shoot." And I just took that opportunity to run and got away. My unregenerated mind didn't recognize this as God's wonderful grace. I said, "Who is he to think that he could pull a gun on me?" And so I went and got a gun myself, and I went back looking for him. I believed that he made me feel to be less of a man.

I wanted him to feel all of those things that I felt. And so, I went to a place where he was known to frequent. As I was walking across the street, I had the gun out and one of the men who was with him saw me first and he reached for his gun. Well, he reached for what I thought would be a gun and I felt I had to defend myself. It was as though I was compelled to do something. I shot him. He died instantly on the spot. I shot another man there who became paralyzed. Once again, I ran to the home of my mother, that praying woman, and she said, "You got to turn yourself in." And I did. I asked her, "I need you to send me a lawyer." And she said, "I'll bring one." But I have to back up, because this lawyer was no lawyer I had ever seen.

A week prior to the time that I shot those men, I was at home and I had this overwhelming internal sensation to get up and do something that I had never done before, and that was to go to church. I didn't even know where a church was, but I found the church where my mother had attended and went there. As I walked in, I saw the *faithful few*, who are the absolute backbone and fiber of the church. My mother was just casually looking around and she saw me in the back of the sanctuary. Her eyes got big and I gave her a look like, "Hey, hey, hey, don't do anything, or I'll leave." So she contained her enthusiasm and a little time went by and the pastor asked if anyone had any prayer requests or any praise reports.

And of course, my mother's hand raised up. "Oh, I do, I do, I do," she said. "Yes, yes. Lady Henry, please share." And so she said, "Well, I have a praise report. The Lord helped me pay a few bills that I didn't know how I was going to pay them and my brakes were bad and the Lord helped me to repair my brakes. And he brought my boy in here. There he is, he's back there."

The pastor did something that I later found out was not traditionally done at midweek Bible study—he made an altar call for anyone who wanted to give their heart to Christ. In that moment, something rose up inside of me that compelled me to go down front and to give my life to Jesus Christ. But I dug in my heels. I didn't respond, but I resolved to come back *next Sunday*—just two, three days away, I can make that. But Saturday was the day of that shooting. That Sunday never came for me, at least not then.

I was involved in that gang shooting and I turned myself in. I told my mother, "I need a lawyer." And she said, "I'm bringing somebody." As it turned out, she brought her pastor. I knew I was in trouble. I was sentenced to 20 years in prison. I thought my life was over as off to prison I went, and back to what I knew best—gangs, drugs, alcohol. I was living like a literal animal in prison with my heart growing cold.

One day a pastor who was popular in the Cleveland area came into the institution. As I walked into that service, a familiar feeling came across me, that same feeling that I felt so many years before. *That following Sunday* had finally come. I felt the presence of God in that service and confessed Jesus Christ as my Lord and my Savior. I wish I could say that from that moment on I walked with the Lord like Enoch. But this was only the beginning of my transformation. I was a Christian, but I didn't like to live like a Christian—I couldn't see past my walls.

A while later, I was involved in a prison drug deal that went bad and was stabbed and left for dead in the prison hospital. I was all bandaged and began to realize that I didn't want to die in prison. It was then that I finally committed my whole self to Christ. Everything about my life changed. I loved it. I was hungry for God's word and began to study the Bible.

God transferred me to another institution where I was called to be in charge of bringing in speakers to the institution, including my mother's pastor and a team from my mother's church. This was the beginning of our ministry to encourage others who had been in various kinds of imprisonment. During that season I met and eventually married my precious wife, Avi Susan. We had begun as pen pals but became partners in life and ministry.

While here at this particular institution, there was a seminary. Winebrenner Theological Seminary in Findlay, Ohio had this radical idea to offer a theological education to the population, and I was blessed to be considered as one of ten men to take part in the program in pastoral studies. I'm now a licensed pastor with the Churches of God General Conference, Great Lakes Division.

Finally, after more than 27 years of incarceration, I was released as a Christian man, as a Christian married man, as a Christian married man who has a calling on his life with a theological education, credentialed, ready to go do work for the Kingdom. And so, the following day we went to get our official paperwork. I was so excited. I was handed my paperwork. I opened it up and it told me that I had not received the parole. And so I took it. I said, "There's a mistake here. I've gotten a parole." And they said, "Oh, let's see." And so they double checked and they took the paper in the back and they came back out. They said, "No, no, no, no, no, you did not receive a parole. In fact, you've been continued for an additional three more years." But God was still working out His plan.

While I was in prison, Avi Susan and I began a ministry called Ever-Growing Ministries. A ministry that really ministered to the heart, to the spiritual and material needs of women who have husbands who are incarcerated. We take every gift God has given us to minister to these families, and one of the most influential gifts that God had given me was my own incarceration. (God has repurposed imprisonment to bring freedom to families in the name of Jesus Christ.)

RELEASING THE WATER FROM THE ROCK

"Behold, I will stand before you there on the rock at Horeb; and you shall strike the rock, and water will come out of it, that the people may drink." And Moses did so in the sight of the elders of Israel (Exodus 17:6).

As we present our wilderness times to God, we learn to trust Him. God provides us with true food and true drink from the Rock, who is Christ Jesus. And so, we move into the realm of the Spirit of God.

VICTORY UNDER GRACE

Then Amalek came and fought against Israel at Rephidim. So Moses said to Joshua, "Choose men

for us and go out, fight against Amalek. Tomor-
row I will station myself on the top of the hill with
the staff of God in my hand." Joshua did as Moses
told him, and fought against Amalek; and Moses,
Aaron, and Hur went up to the top of the hill. So
it came about when Moses held his hand up, that
Israel prevailed, and when he let his hand down,
Amalek prevailed. But Moses' hands were heavy.
Then they took a stone and put it under him, and
he sat on it; and Aaron and Hur supported his
hands, one on one side and one on the other. Thus
his hands were steady until the sun set. So Joshua
overwhelmed Amalek and his people with the
edge of the sword (Exodus 17:8-13).

This victory is a picture of God's grace. Moses stationed himself on the rock, the Mercy Seat of Christ. Aaron, whose name means "bringer of light" or "truth," and Joshua, whose name means "salvation," are the cherubim on the Mercy Seat, the cherubim that held up Moses' arms as he clasped the staff, God's repurposing grace. That glorious grace was the proof that God had appeared to Moses! In community today, we position ourselves on the Mercy Seat of Christ while our brothers and sisters hold up our arms (or we hold up theirs) in order that they or we may clasp the repurposing grace of God on our journey through life.

GRACE OVER WORKS

God is in the habit of doing the seemingly impossible, or at least what is impossible to us. All of this He does by His grace. In the battle against the Amalekites, Moses held up his staff, the repurposing grace of God, over his head. Amalek was a descendent of Esau, a man of carnality. The root of the word Amalek is Amal which means "works" or toil or labor. As long as the staff, the repurposing grace of God, was held over his head, Moses triumphed over Amalek, over works or mere religion. God was present in the battle and Moses again stood still and saw God win.

So then, this is an important lesson—that grace triumphs over works. This is the final point. In order for God to repurpose our challenges, difficulties, failures, we must rely on the grace of God. And, as I stated previously, we must see that God is up to something more than we know. We must turn aside to see what God's purpose is. We must open ourselves to that purpose and present our sticks to God so that we will free captives, go through impossible obstacles, bring water out of a rock, and find victory under grace.

God's repurposing grace is our salvation and our freedom. "It was for (true) freedom that Christ set us free." (Gal. 5:1) Like the song says….

Praying for a miracle
Thirsty for the living well
Only You can satisfy
Sweetness at the mercy seat
Now I've tasted, it's not hard to see
Only You can satisfy

There's honey in the rock...
...Freedom where the Spirit is
Bounty in the wilderness
You will always satisfy, yeah[1]

TURNING ASIDE

Tremble, O earth, at the presence of the Lord, at the presence of the God of Jacob. He turned the rock into a pool of water; yes, a spring of water flowed from solid rock (Psalm 114:7-8 NLT).

1. Back to the first question at the beginning of this chapter: Have you ever been really thirsty? What is the rock that you are dealing with right now?

_____

_____

_____

_____

_____

_____

_____

1   Author's note: It is suggested you listen to this song before reading the next chapters You Tube Link

2. Take a few minutes and write down places where you feel stuck between a rock and a hard place (places that seem to be hard as a rock), where there appears to be no life.

3. Now put yourself in that situation, in front of that rocky place. Acknowledge the presence of the Lord in that place.

_____

_____

_____

_____

_____

- Now, See that God might be up to something in your circumstance, even as He was up to something in Torriano's three extra years in prison.

- Turn aside from your normal way of thinking.

- Take off your sandals and Open yourself to God's presence.

- Now Present yourself, your whole self, to the purpose of God in your situation. God has a plan.

CHAPTER EIGHT

UNTIL

To You I lift up my eyes,
O You who are enthroned in the heavens!
Behold, as the eyes of servants
look to the hand of their master,
As the eyes of a maid to
the hand of her mistress,
So our eyes look to the Lord our God,
Until He is gracious to us.

(Psalm 123: 1-2, NAS)

In the previous chapters, we've talked much about going through challenges and difficult times and finding God's purpose in the midst of them. In short, to repurpose them. An unfolding has yet to take place. This unfolding could be summarized in the word until! Until is the distance from here to there, from now until then. The psalm above tells us that we must look to the throne of God and wait for the until of His repurposing grace.

The word "wait" is implied: we wait "until He is gracious…" Two words we might have difficulty with are the words *wait* and *until*, yet they are tied together. The word *wait* is often seen in the Hebrew Scriptures and is a word that is first mentioned in Genesis 1:9: "*Then God said, 'Let the waters below the heavens be gathered into one place, and let the dry land appear'; and it was so.*" The Hebrew word for "wait" is *qavah*. It means "all of me needs to be gathered together in the presence of God." The Hebrew word for "until" is *ad*. *Ad* appears many times in the Hebrew Scriptures and the feeling of the word is something like "yet to appear." My will must be "woven together" with His. We always seem to want something to happen suddenly, but *suddenly* is simply a very brief *until*. Regardless, the timing and purpose belong to God. So we look to the throne and we *wait until* our purpose is completely interwoven with His.

> *But those who wait for the Lord [who expect, look for, and hope in Him] shall change and renew their strength and power; they shall lift their wings and mount up [close to God] as eagles*

[mount up to the sun]; they shall run and not be weary, they shall walk and not faint or become tired (Isaiah 40:31 AMPC).

Until is a season.

It involves a goal or the fullness of time. "You can't have dessert *until* you clean your plate." "You can't vote *until* you're 21." When we face an *until*, we want to look back, around, down, forward, everywhere but to the One enthroned. *Until* is a time of growth—a growth of trust in God.

Until is not passive.

It's like an army waiting for an order to attack. They're prepared and ready but cannot attach *until* the order is given. We don't do well with *until*. We are better with *now*. We are all in some kind of *until* many times. There are *untils* of sickness, finances, etc. We are in an *until* right now.

Untils are part of God's plan.

Consider that *untils* are part of God's plan. They move us toward the goal like a rest in a musical theme. A rest is a pause when there seems to be nothing happening, but it's actually part of the melody. It helps us anticipate the next note.

Until seems dark, but: *The Light shines in the darkness, and the darkness did not comprehend it* (John 1:5).

If I say, "Surely the darkness will overwhelm me, and the light around me will be night, even the darkness is not dark to You, and the night is as bright as the day. Darkness and light are alike to You" (Psalm 139:11-12).

It is He who reveals the profound and hidden things; He knows what is in the darkness (Daniel 2:22).

Light arises in the darkness for the upright; He is gracious and compassionate and righteous (Psalm 112:4).

He will guide us:

I will lead the blind by a way they do not know, in paths they do not know I will guide them. I will make darkness into light before them and rugged places into plains. These are the things I will do, and I will not leave them undone (Isaiah 42:16).

Again, *until* can seem like a dark place, but the One who is enthroned is most creative in the dark. Creation itself was an *until.* Elohim created; the Spirit vibrated over darkness *until* God said, "Let there be Light.'"That Light was Christ. Even in the face of our *untils,* the Spirit is already moving. He is vibrating all over that "until" *until* Christ is seen. So perhaps when we face an *until* of whatever duration, we should declare, "Let there be light."

We experience many *untils* in our lives. Psalm 123 above was composed regarding people who were experiencing great pressure. They were a people who had things put in order, yet were surrounded by enemies oppressing them. You and I also may have most things right, and our lives well put in place, yet we still inevitably face problems and opposition. Our ears may ring with the echoes of past failures or present difficulties. When we are faced with these difficulties, we often ask "Why" or "Why me?" The problem with those questions is that we exit the realm of the Spirit and the presence of God, and we enter into our own mind and reasoning. Our thoughts, then, become obstacles to God's repurposing grace.

If we would recall 2 Chronicles 20, we would see a similar sentiment to Psalm 123 when the king makes a statement: "Lord, we don't know what to do, but our eyes are on You." Led by the Spirit of God, the king commanded the most unreasonable battle strategy. He commanded that his army would go out, but with the praise team in front. Beloved, it was the praise of God that overcame the assault of three enemy armies! When confronted with an *until*, we also must gather all of ourselves together in the presence of God and look to Him in confidence and praise.

Sometimes an *until* seems like a vast, unnavigable, roiling ocean. Such was the case of Moses and Israel at the Red Sea with the Egyptians behind them and the sea before them. But recall Moses' instruction that they were to stand still and let God fight for them. The Red Sea was their *until*—but the Spirit of God was already moving. All night long the wind, or Spirit, was making a way before them and would destroy the enemy behind them. We could also note that when the people of Israel were thirsty, that very thirst was another *until*. The thirst prepared them to see a miraculous supply of refreshing water—from a rock, of all things!

The *untils* of life are holy ground. Even as Moses had to remove his sandals on holy ground, so our *untils* are the holy ground where we remove our own human understanding and seek the face of God. There God will speak to us. He will tell us who He is, who we are, and our next move. He sees our life through an eternal, timeless perspective. God calls our name, as He did with Moses, and we say with Moses, "Behold, here I am, Lord."

WHAT DO WE DO WITH UNTILS?

Until requires the attitude of a servant. Servants watch, wait, trust, and prepare. As we wait on the Lord and He renews us, we are woven together with Him.

What did Abraham do *until* he saw the covenant promises of God fulfilled? Genesis tells us:

> *Then the Lord appeared to Abram and said, "To your offspring I will give this land." So he built there an altar to the Lord, who had appeared to him. From there he moved to the hill country on the east of Bethel and pitched his tent, with*

Bethel on the west and Ai on the east. And there he built an altar to the Lord and called upon the name of the Lord (Genesis 12:7-8 ESV).

1. He pitched his tent with Bethel on the west and Ai on the east.

Bethel represents communion with God; Ai represents something like confusion, perhaps darkness. This is where we may find ourselves with an *until*. Many times we live somewhere between communion and confusion. A tent is a temporary dwelling. It is not eternal. We must realize our *untils* are temporary—where we live right now. God is moving us forward.

2   And there he built an altar to the Lord and...

An altar is a place of covenant where we are affirming God's presence and purpose. It is a place of trust.

3. He called upon the name of the Lord.

Calling on the name of the Lord is worship. Our *untils* are a place of worship.

Christ reigns in our *untils*. Christ is the light that will be revealed in our *until*. From the beginning of the Torah to the end of Revelation 21, Christ is the light.

But He, having offered one sacrifice for sins for all time, sat down at the right hand of God, waiting from that time onward until His enemies be made a footstool for His feet (Hebrews 10:12-14; see also Psalm 110; Acts 2:34).

Beloved, God is a repurposing God. He is the artist of creation. In our *untils,* we are submitting to the hand of the artist. *We look to the hand of God as His servants and we wait* until *He is gracious to us.*

> *For yet the vision [is] for a season,*
> *and it breathes for the end,*
> *and does not lie,*
> *if it lingers,*
> *wait for it,*
> *for surely it comes,*
> *it is not late*
> (Habakkuk 2:3 LSV).

TURNING ASIDE

Where or what is your until? Settle yourself in the presence of God and consider your untils.

_____

_____

_____

_____

_____

_____

1. Pitch your tent in this place. Realize this is temporary, and God is moving you forward.

2. Build an altar here and affirm your trust in God in the face of your "until."

3. Now compose a prayer of trust and entrust your until into the hands of Jesus.

....

....

....

....

....

....

....

....

....

4. Take time now to worship and commit yourself to the repurposing grace of God.

To You I lift up my eyes, O You who are enthroned in the heavens! Behold, as the eyes of servants look to the hand of their master, as the eyes of a maid to the hand of her mistress, so our eyes look to the Lord our God, until He is gracious to us (Psalm 123:1-2).

CHAPTER NINE

FINDING GOD IN THE WILDERNESS

Therefore, say to the people of Israel: 'I am the LORD, I will free you from your oppression and will rescue from your slavery in Egypt. I will redeem you with a powerful arm and great acts of judgement (toward Egypt) (Exodus 6:6 NLT 2nd ed.).

God's Divine Purposing

God repurposes our suffering and challenges so...[1]

Do any of these scriptures, phrases, or words apply to your circumstances? Underline words or phrases that apply to you personally. Turn the applicable words or phrases into a praise to God and write it on the lines below or in your journal.

—so we will turn to Him.

> *For many days Israel was without the true God and without a teaching priest and without law. But in their distress they turned to the Lord God of Israel, and they sought Him, and He let them find Him* (2 Chronicles 15:3-4).

—to incite us to search for Him.

> *O Lord, they sought You in distress; they could only whisper a prayer, Your chastening was upon them* (Isaiah 26:16).

—to develop patience and endurance.

> *Therefore, having been justified by faith, we have peace with God through our Lord Jesus Christ, through whom also we have obtained our introduction by faith into this grace in which we*

stand; and we exult in hope of the glory of God.
And not only this, but we also exult in our trib-
ulations, knowing that tribulation brings about
perseverance; and perseverance, proven charac-
ter; and proven character, hope; and hope does
not disappoint, because the love of God has been
poured out within our hearts through the Holy
Spirit who was given to us (Romans 5:1-5).

**—to refine us and make us into the people He
wants us to be.**

Blessed be the God and Father of our Lord
Jesus Christ, who according to His great mercy
has caused us to be born again to a living hope

through the resurrection of Jesus Christ from the dead, to obtain an inheritance which is imperishable and undefiled and will not fade away, reserved in heaven for you, who are protected by the power of God through faith for a salvation ready to be revealed in the last time. In this you greatly rejoice, even though now for a little while, if necessary, you have been distressed by various trials, so that the proof of your faith, being more precious than gold which is perishable, even though tested by fire, may be found to result in praise and glory and honor at the revelation of Jesus Christ; and though you have not seen Him, you love Him, and though you do not see Him now, but believe in Him, you greatly rejoice with joy inexpressible and full of glory, obtaining as the outcome of your faith the salvation of your souls (1 Peter 1:3-9).

—to expose our weaknesses and cause us to rely on His power.

> *Because of the surpassing greatness of the revelations, for this reason, to keep me from exalting myself, there was given me a thorn in the flesh, a messenger of Satan to torment me—to keep me from exalting myself! Concerning this I implored the Lord three times that it might leave me. And He has said to me, "My grace is sufficient for you, for power is perfected in weakness." Most gladly, therefore, I will rather boast about my weaknesses, so that the power of Christ may dwell in me. Therefore I am well content with weaknesses, with insults, with distresses, with persecutions, with difficulties, for Christ's sake; for when I am weak, then I am strong* (2 Corinthians 12:7-10).

—*in order for us to be mature and become complete.*

> *Consider it all joy, my brethren, when you encounter various trials, knowing that the testing of your faith produces endurance. And let endurance have its perfect result, so that you may be perfect and complete, lacking in nothing* (James 1:2-4).

_____

_____

_____

_____

_____

_____

_____

—to spread the gospel.

> *Now I want you to know, brethren, that my circumstances have turned out for the greater progress of the gospel, so that my imprisonment in the cause of Christ has become well known throughout the whole praetorian guard and to everyone else, and that most of the brethren, trusting in the Lord because of my imprisonment, have far more courage to speak the word of God without fear* (Philippians 1:12-14).

_____

_____

_____

_____

—so that His power may be displayed in our life.

> *As He passed by, He saw a man blind from birth. And His disciples asked Him, "Rabbi, who sinned this man or his parents, that he would be born blind?" Jesus answered, "It was neither that this man sinned, nor his parents; but it was so that the works of God might be displayed in him. We must work the works of Him who sent Me as long as it is day; night is coming when no one can work. While I am in the world, I am the Light of the world"* (John 9:1-5).

_____

_____

_____

_____

_____

_____

_____

—to become worthy of God's Kingdom.

This is a plain indication of God's righteous judgment so that you will be considered worthy of the kingdom of God, for which indeed you are suffering (2 Thessalonians 1:5).

_____

_____

_____

_____

_____

_____

_____

_____

—to learn from our mistakes and keep us focused on Him.

Teach me good discernment and knowledge, for I believe in Your commandments. Before I was afflicted I went astray, but now I keep Your word (Psalm 119:66-67).

—so that we can show compassion to others who are suffering.

> *Blessed be the God and Father of our Lord Jesus Christ, the Father of mercies and God of all comfort, who comforts us in all our affliction so that we will be able to comfort those who are in any affliction with the comfort with which we ourselves are comforted by God. For just as the sufferings of Christ are ours in abundance, so also our comfort is abundant through Christ* (2 Corinthians 1:3-5).

—to give us the opportunity to make known that we are servants of God.

> *You also became imitators of us and of the Lord, having received the word in much tribulation*

with the joy of the Holy Spirit, so that you became an example to all the believers in Macedonia and in Achaia (1 Thessalonians 1:6-7).

—————————————————————————

—————————————————————————

—————————————————————————

—————————————————————————

—————————————————————————

—————————————————————————

—————————————————————————

—————————————————————————

—to have an appreciation of true happiness.

For His anger is but for a moment, His favor is for a lifetime; weeping may last for the night, but a shout of joy comes in the morning (Psalm 30:5).

—————————————————————————

—————————————————————————

—————————————————————————

All discipline for the moment seems not to be joyful, but sorrowful; yet to those who have been trained by it, afterwards it yields the peaceful fruit of righteousness (Hebrews 12:11).

GOD'S DIVINE EXCHANGE

God has redemption in His heart toward us. There's much evidence in the scriptures of God's repurposing grace I love the chorus of this song by the Elevation worship team, "Graves Into Gardens." (Carol and I listen to this nearly every morning to remind ourselves of the potential of God's repurposing for the day ahead.) You may want to write the Scriptures that apply to you and underline words or phrases that apply to you as suggested in the previous part of this chapter.

You turn mourning to dancing

> *You have turned for me my mourning into dancing; You have loosed my sackcloth and girded me with gladness* (Psalm 30:11).

You give beauty for ashes

To grant those who mourn in Zion, giving them a garland instead of ashes, the oil of gladness instead of mourning, the mantle of praise instead of a spirit of fainting. So they will be called oaks of righteousness, the planting of the Lord, that He may be glorified (Isaiah 61:3).

You turn shame into glory

Behold, I am going to deal at that time With all your oppressors, I will save the lame And gather the outcast, And I will turn their shame into praise and renown In all the earth (Zephaniah 3:19).

You turn graves into gardens

Therefore prophesy and say to them, "Thus says the Lord God, 'Behold, I will open your graves and cause you to come up out of your graves, My people; and I will bring you into the land of Israel. Then you will know that I am the Lord, when I have opened your graves and caused you to come up out of your graves, My people. I will put My Spirit within you and you will come to life, and I will place you on your own land. Then you will know that I, the Lord, have spoken and done it,' declares the Lord" (Ezekiel 37:12-14).

_____

_____

_____

_____

_____

_____

_____

_____

You turn bones into armies

> *Then He said to me, "Prophesy to the breath, prophesy, son of man, and say to the breath, 'Thus says the Lord God, "Come from the four winds, O breath, and breathe on these slain, that they come to life."' So I prophesied as He commanded me, and the breath came into them, and they came to life and stood on their feet, an exceedingly great army* (Ezekiel 37:9-10).

_____

_____

_____

_____

You turn seas into highways

Then Moses stretched out his hand over the sea; and the Lord swept the sea back by a strong east wind all night and turned the sea into dry land, so the waters were divided. The sons of Israel went through the midst of the sea on the dry land, and the waters were like a wall to them on their right hand and on their left (Exodus 14:21-22).

You're the only one who can

> *But Moses said to the people, "Do not fear! Stand by and see the salvation of the Lord which He will accomplish for you today; for the Egyptians whom you have seen today, you will never see them again forever. The Lord will fight for you while you keep silent"* (Exodus 14:13-14).

_____

_____

_____

_____

_____

_____

_____

_____

_____

_____

He's the only one who can.

NOTE

1. This list was compiled by Pastor Ed Jelliff of New Life Alliance Church, East Freedom, PA.

ABOUT THOM GARDNER

Thom Gardner has a passion to see people grow in the abundant life Jesus promised us. Thom earned a DMin focused on spiritual formation from Winebrenner Theological Seminary and has authored several books focused on healing and growth in Christ. He has served as a teacher, pastor, formational counselor and adjunct professor of Spiritual Formation and pastoral care. As president of Restored Life Ministries, Thom and his wife Carol travel internationally offering equipping classes and retreats focused on healing and spiritual growth.

www.restoredlifeministries.com

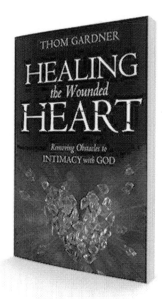

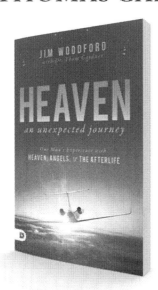

From

THOM GARDNER

The Lord is abundant in mercy to all who call upon Him. Jesus was mercy-in-person when He walked on the earth. But how can mercy be like honeysuckle? Just as honeysuckle vines overcome fences, God's mercy has the power to grow relentlessly in our hearts, conquering all kinds of obstacles that result from our wounded human relationships and limited human reason.

As you read and reflect on the scriptural revelations, you'll discover the life-changing truth that mercy *is* the Passion, the Presence, and the Glory of God. "Turning Points" at the end of each chapter will guide you through prayer and journaling to help you **feel** the passion, **experience** the presence, and **see** the glory of God as you comprehend God's *Relentless Love* for you.

Ultimately, as you receive His mercy you will be empowered to show mercy to those around you – even those who've wounded you.

Made in the USA
Middletown, DE
25 March 2023

27160333R00091